# GLOBETROTTER™

## Travel Guide

# MOZAMBIQUE

## MIKE SLATER

NEW
HOLLAND

NEW
HOLLAND

★★★ Highly recommended
★★ Recommended
★ See if you can

Third edition published in 2006
by New Holland Publishers (UK) Ltd
London • Cape Town • Sydney • Auckland
First published in 1997

10 9 8 7 6 5 4 3 2 1

www.newhollandpublishers.com

Garfield House, 86 Edgware Road
London W2 2EA
United Kingdom

80 McKenzie Street
Cape Town 8001
South Africa

14 Aquatic Drive
Frenchs Forest, NSW 2086
Australia

218 Lake Road
Northcote, Auckland
New Zealand

Distributed in the USA by
The Globe Pequot Press
Connecticut

ISBN 1 84537 580 7

**Publishing Manager:** Thea Grobbelaar
**DTP Cartographic Manager:** Genené Hart
**Editors:** Thea Grobbelaar, Melany McCallum,
Claudia Dos Santos
**Picture Researchers:** Shavonne Govender,
Sonya Cupido
**Design and DTP:** Nicole Bannister, Sonya Cupido

**Cartographers:** Tanja Spinola, Marisa Galloway,
William Smuts
**Compiler:** Elaine Fick
Reproduction by Hirt & Carter (Pty) Ltd, Cape Town
Printed and bound by Times Offset (M) Sdn. Bhd., Malaysia

Although every effort has been made to ensure that this
guide is up to date and current at time of going to print,
the Publisher accepts no responsibility or liability for any
loss, injury or inconvenience incurred by readers or
travellers using this guide.

**Keep us Current**
Information in travel guides is apt to change, which is
why we regularly update our guides. We'd be grateful to
receive feedback if you've noted something we should
include in our updates. If you have new information,
please share it with us by writing to the Publishing
Manager, Globetrotter, at the office nearest to you
(addresses on this page). The most significant
contribution to each new edition will receive a free
copy of the updated guide.

**Photographic Credits:**
**Anthony Bannister Photo Library/Andrew Bannister**,
pages 11, 25, 64, 83, 91; **Gerald Cubitt**, pages 9, 10;
**Peter Kirchhoff**, pages 14, 34; **Photo Access (*Getaway*)/
Jackie Nel**, pages 19, 33 (top), 44; **Photo Access
(*Getaway*)/David Steele**, title page, pages 4, 8, 21, 27,
28, 47, 50, 55, 80, 81 (top and bottom); **Photo Access
(*Getaway*)/Patrick Wagner**, pages 7, 18, 38, 49, 76;
**Mike Slater**, cover, pages 17, 20, 22, 30, 33 (bottom),
35, 36, 40, 41, 48, 51–53, 58, 66–69, 71–73, 82, 85,
92, 94, 95, 96 (top), 99, 102, 109–117; **Ariadne van
Zandbergen**, pages 6, 13, 15, 23, 24, 26, 29, 37, 39, 54,
61–63, 65, 70, 78, 79, 88, 93, 96 (bottom), 97, 100, 101,
103, 106, 118 (top and bottom), 119.

**Acknowledgements:**
The author wishes to thank:
Carrie of www.linksmoz.com
Richard of www.mozoo.co.mz
Paul Dutton, Michelle of Chirabeze Lda, and Kate and
Mariette of Quinta Capricórnio, Lichinga, for their invalu-
able input of information and insight. For the history sec-
tion of this book, extensive reference was made to Malyn
Newitt's *A History of Mozambique* (see page 126).

**Front Cover:** *Drinks are served at Benguerra Lodge.*
**Title Page:** *Sport fishing boat, Benguerra Island.*

# CONTENTS

# 1
# Introducing Mozambique

From the overgrown remnants of **Portuguese outposts** along the mighty Zambezi to the ancient, mysterious **Mwenu Mutapa kingdom** and the enchanting and unique **Mozambique Island**, Mozambique offers an enticing and fascinating blend of cultures.

**Arab dhows** and modern **speedboats** crisscross the translucent tropical waters of a coral-fringed coastline, where **scuba-diving** opportunities rival the world's best. One of the lasting legacies of **Portuguese** and **Arab** traders and colonists are the colourful settlements found along the coast. Maputo, Inhambane, Beira, Quelimane and Pemba display a variety of architectural styles – from **Manueline** (see p. 27) to gaudy 1930s-inspired **Art Deco**.

So far, fortune-seekers have failed in their quest to find the legendary mines of **King Solomon**, said to contain hoards of gold, yet the stunning diversity of coastal, riverine, mountain and forest environments are Mozambique's real treasure trove – home to a splendid array of fauna and flora, interspersed with traditional villages.

Neglected during the civil upheaval, the **Gorongosa National Park**, **Maputo Elephant Reserve**, **Bazaruto National Park** and the **Niassa Reserve** are being rehabilitated, while tropical island gems like **Benguerra**, **Bazaruto** and the remote **Quirimbas** offer seclusion, luxurious accommodation and excellent diving, fishing and bird-watching.

Whether you find yourself on one of the endless deserted beaches or diving off the **coral isles**, you will discover a country filled with the enchanting sights and soothing sounds of Africa.

## TOP ATTRACTIONS

★★★ **Bazaruto Archipelago:** luxury lodges and virgin reefs away from the crowds.
★★★ **Maputaland:** migrating elephants; dive with dolphins.
★★ **Ilha de Moçambique (Mozambique Island):** 16th-century Portuguese fortress in an intact Swahili/Portuguese city with a timeless ambience.
★★ **Pomene beach:** sweeping sands, tidal pools, caves, catch game fish off the rocks.
★★ **Inhambane Town:** the most pleasant settlement on the coast of East Africa.

**Opposite:** *Coral reefs are accessible from the derelict hotel on Magaruque Island.*

**Right:** *Mount Namúli, Mozambique's second-highest mountain.*
**Opposite:** *Snorkelling in the crystal water of the 'aquarium' off Benguerra Island's Two-Mile Reef.*

---

### THE ZAMBEZI DELTA

• Width: 100km (62 miles) from Micaùne in the north to Rio Múngari in the south.
• Area: the river divides at Chupanga; the delta covers 4000km² (1544 sq miles).
• Steam engines: the sugar plantations were served by a narrow-gauge railway until 1978. The system now lies derelict, but the steam engines on the tracks near Chinde and Marromeu await inspection by enthusiasts.

---

### VITAL STATISTICS

• Location: Between 26°52′S–21°27′S and 30°31′E–40°51′E.
• Area: 799,380km² (308,561 sq miles).
• Highest point: Mt Binga, 2436m (7993ft).
• Highest-lying province: Niassa; lowest is Sofala.
• Warmest town: Tete (28°C; 82°F); coolest town is Lichinga (18°C; 64°F).
• Longest river: Zambezi; length in Mozambique is 820km (510 miles).
• Largest bay: Pemba, at 375km² (144 sq miles).
• Deepest harbour: Nacala, at 300m (984ft).

---

## THE LAND

Mozambique borders on South Africa and Swaziland to the south, Zimbabwe to the west and Zambia and Malawi in the northwest. The Rovuma River forms the remote boundary with Tanzania. The Indian Ocean's Mozambique Channel flanks a splendid coastline which is over 2500km (1554 miles) long. The south of the country is characterized by the extensive, well-treed savanna of the **Mozambican Plain**, where altitudes rarely range above 200m (656ft). The **Mozambican Plateau** dominates the central and northern regions, where rugged highlands are deeply incised by river valleys, and peaks such as **Binga** and **Gorongosa** in Manica, **Chiperone** in Zambézia, **Namúli** in Nampula and **Malema** in Niassa are located.

Most of Mozambique's tourist destinations are located along the southern coastline, or tucked away on islands such as **Inhaca** and the unique **Bazaruto Archipelago**, yet the interior, from the hot springs of Zambézia province and the granite domes of Nampula to the **Gorongosa forests** and **Quissico lakes**, is not without its attractions.

### Mountains and Rivers

Mozambique is cleft by the wide valley of the languid **Zambezi River**, which has gathered runoff from five countries and coursed over 3000km (1864 miles) before entering Mozambique at Feira. Here it is temporarily tamed by the 270km (168-mile) **Lake Cahora Bassa**, with its 160m (525ft) dam wall and the potential to generate 4000 megawatts of hydroelectricity. Below the dam wall the river passes under the bridges at Tete and Sena before dispersing some 600km (373 miles) downstream into the myriad channels of its 100km (62-mile) wide delta.

Other major rivers that flow through Mozambique are the crocodile-infested **Incomáti**, **Limpopo** and **Save** in the south and the **Licungo**, **Ligonha**, **Lúrio**, **Lugenda** and **Rovuma** in the north. The latter is noteworthy: not only does it form Mozambique's frontier with Tanzania, it also remains a formidable barrier. It isn't spanned by a single bridge and only recently has a ferry at the mouth afforded overland access to or from the north – crossings of the Rovuma are otherwise possible by canoe only.

The 2436m (7993ft) **Binga Peak** in the Chimanimani sandstone range ranks as Mozambique's highest mountain, while the granite crags of **Mount Malema** in Niassa present a challenge even to the most accomplished rock-climber. Religious ceremonies take place in caves on the slopes of **Mount Namúli** in Zambézia. In northern Tete province, which is notorious for its sticky tropical climate, the slopes of **Mount Dómuè** and the **Moravian Plateau** provide welcome relief from the oppressive heat.

### Seas and Shores

Over 1200 species of fish have been identified in the coastal waters of Mozambique, most of which inhabit the extensive **coral reefs** that line the coast, particularly off **Maputaland**, around **Inhaca Island**, in the region of **Inhambane** and **Pebane** and along the **Quirimba Archipelago** in the far north. Kingfish, mackerel, and tuna, a vital link in the food chain of the ocean and a popular catch with the locals, are attracted to the nourishment provided by the corals and their associated sea

> **MOUNTAINS OF MYSTERY**
>
> • **Gorongosa:** a wonderland of diverse habitats; home to an oustanding variety of rare birds including green-headed orioles, buntings and canaries.
> • **Chiperone:** named for the icy winds that blow off its summit, this peak rises out of a steamy, trackless jungle.
> • **Namúli:** animists pay tribute to spirits in the hidden caves near the summit.
> • **Malema:** in a remote part of Nampula Province; a climber's challenge of sheer granite walls and precipitous exposed cliffs.
> • **Binga:** Mozambique's highest point, straddling the border with Zimbabwe.

## PLEISTOCENE PONDS

Mozambique's **coastal lakes** were formed during the Pleistocene epoch, when marine gullies were gradually lifted above the surface of the sea, becoming exposed to the atmosphere after giant sections of the earth's crust tilted. Longshore drift and wave and wind action slowly added material to the seaward banks, building them up into some of the world's highest **sand dunes**. Today the lakes would be dry if it were not for the ground water seeping up through the sand. The water in the lakes remains **brackish** and unpleasant to drink.

**Opposite:** *Storm clouds gather over Gorongosa National Park.*
**Below:** *Atmospheric sunsets like this are common at Benguerra Island Lodge.*

life. In terms of the variety of marine organisms, Mozambique's reefs are on a par with Australia's magnificent Great Barrier Reef, except that they are far less crowded and commercialized. Mozambique's superb reefs are delicate and as yet unspoilt marine wildernesses, their beauty and commercial value increasing the urgent need for formal protection.

South of the **Save River**, the coast is characterized by a string of inland lakes not fed by rivers and cut off from the sea by high parabolic (bowl-shaped) dunes stabilized by vegetation. The largest expanses of water in this coastal lake zone are lakes **Uembje** (Bilene), **Quissico** and **Inharrime**. Travellers on the main road between Maputo and Inhambane will be treated to scenic views from convenient vantage points.

## Climate

Two major factors influencing Mozambique's climate are the warm Indian Ocean current moving south from the equator, and the altitude of the Mozambican Plateau. Temperatures along the coast and in the lower-lying areas of the plain and the Zambezi valley increase as one moves further north. Mozambique experiences **rain** mainly during **November–April**, while **August** is the **driest** month in most areas. The **wettest** provinces are **Niassa** (Metangula receives 300mm, or 12in, during

March) and **Cabo Delgado** (Pemba receives some 260mm, or 10in, between December and February). The **driest** part of the country is **Pafúri** in Gaza Province where average annual precipitation rarely reaches 300mm (12in).

| COMPARATIVE CLIMATE CHART | MAPUTO | | | | BEIRA | | | | LICHINGA | | | |
|---|---|---|---|---|---|---|---|---|---|---|---|---|
| | SUM | AUT | WIN | SPR | SUM | AUT | WIN | SPR | SUM | AUT | WIN | SPR |
| | JAN | APR | JULY | OCT | JAN | APR | JULY | OCT | JAN | APR | JULY | OCT |
| MAX TEMP. °C | 31 | 25 | 21 | 25 | 34 | 29 | 22 | 27 | 25 | 20 | 19 | 23 |
| MIN TEMP. | 27 | 21 | 18 | 20 | 29 | 26 | 19 | 23 | 20 | 16 | 12 | 20 |
| MAX TEMP. °F | 88 | 77 | 70 | 77 | 93 | 84 | 72 | 81 | 77 | 68 | 66 | 73 |
| MIN TEMP. °F | 81 | 70 | 64 | 68 | 84 | 79 | 66 | 73 | 68 | 61 | 54 | 68 |
| RAINFALL in | 3 | 2 | 1.5 | 1.5 | 6 | 4 | 0.9 | 0.7 | 5 | 3 | 0.4 | 0 |
| RAINFALL mm | 75 | 55 | 40 | 40 | 144 | 110 | 25 | 20 | 120 | 80 | 10 | 0 |

## Tropical Cyclones

The tropical cyclone is one of the most powerful and potentially destructive forms of atmospheric circulation. Falling just outside the region between 8°S and 15°S, where the Indian Ocean temperatures are above 27°C (81°F), the **Mozambique Channel** experiences tropical cyclones every few years, few of which move further south than Beira. The most recent cyclones that have wreaked destruction on Mozambique were **Eline** and **Gloria** in 2000.

## Plant Life

Much of Mozambique's temperate rainforests such as the ones around Dondo, Nova Vanduzi and Gogói have been devastated by logging and slash-and-burn agriculture. Yet magnificent **mopane woodlands** still dominate the southern plains, where battered old **baobab trees** flourish around Funhalouro in Inhambane province and along the northern coastline. Both species are important food sources: protein-rich mopane worms are widely eaten, while young baobabs are edible in their entirety.

The **woodland mahogany**, or *nkuhlu*, is widely distributed throughout Mozambique. Its spread is often greater than its height and can sometimes be seen to shelter an entire African *kraal* (homestead).

**Right:** *Impala in the Gorongosa National Park.*
**Opposite:** Padrãos *(stone pillars) like this one were erected by da Gama.*

## Wildlife

Although the devastation of Mozambique's wildlife is unprecedented in Africa in recent times, programmes to reintroduce those species which attract tourists are now gathering momentum. **Elephant** can be viewed in the extreme south (Fúti channel), and in the far north along the banks of the Rovuma River in the Niassa Reserve. **Buffalo**, **lion**, **leopard**, **roan** and **sable** exist, albeit in relatively small and threatened numbers, in the Gorongosa and Zambezi delta regions.

Peace Parks straddling Mozambique's borders, such as the **Great Limpopo Transfrontier Reserve** (www.great limpopopark.com/), are now open.

Mozambique's bird life is exceptional. Over 900 species have been spotted south of the Zambezi. The best viewing spots are the Mount Gorongosa and National Park region, Gurúè and Milange in Zambézia, Metangula and Cobúè in Niassa, Panda in Gaza and in the Maputo Elephant Reserve.

## Conserving Mozambique's Natural Heritage

The pitiful state of **Gorongosa National Park** is indicative of the desperate position of Mozambique's fauna. Of six proclaimed parks in Mozambique (Limpopo, Banhine, Zinave, Gorongosa, Bazaruto Archipelago, Gili and Niassa) only Limpopo, Gorongosa, Niassa and the Archipelago are ready to receive visitors. The **Elephant Reserve** across Maputo Bay may be visited but, while there is a rustic camp site at Ponta Milibangalala, there are no permanent facilities.

# HISTORY IN BRIEF

About 2000 years ago, climatic shifts caused the Sahara Desert of North Africa to expand southward, triggering a wave of **migration** from northwest Africa through the equatorial regions to southeast Africa. Northern Bantu-speaking tribes clashed with the nomadic hunter-gatherers of the south and displaced them. By the time (around AD300) **Arab traders** first landed on Mozambique's offshore islands, the aboriginal mainland inhabitants had been absorbed into Bantu society. Muslim traders, masters of the nuances of African trade and cultural practices, established alliances with tribes through intermarriage.

**Vasco da Gama** is generally honoured as the 'discoverer' of Mozambique. The span of coast which his small fleet of four vessels passed on Christmas Day 1497 was named **Natal**. Early in 1498 he anchored off an estuary near Inharrime in what is now Inhambane province.

From AD300–1500, none of the Indian Ocean powers maintained a fleet, and so they were helpless when Portuguese warships arrived at Sofala and Mozambique Island in the early 16th century. After erecting a fort here, Portuguese soldiers began demanding 'duties' on the cloth, ivory and gold leaving the area.

## The Mwenu Mutapa

Portuguese traders were largely ignorant of the interior, but desperately desired to eclipse Spanish successes in the Americas, and so fabricated the myth of a fabulously rich empire which they called **Monomotapa,** after its leader, the Mwenu Mutapa. During the 18th century it was not so much the promise of untold wealth that motivated the Portuguese crown to pacify the tribes of the interior, but rather the murders of several missionaries and traders.

**SOSHANGANE, FATHER OF A NATION**

For centuries Southern Mozambique has been the home of the **Tsonga**; the origins of the **Shangaan** nation, however, lie in the more recent past. During the wars of Zulu king **Shaka**, Chief Soshangane and his people fled into Mozambique, where they clashed with and conquered the **Ronga** tribe. Though his warriors were not in the same league as Shaka's *impi*, Soshangane surprised himself by defeating a Zulu army that had crossed the Pongola River in 1828. The battle spelt disaster for Shaka who was murdered by his half-brother that same year. Soshangane's spears, by contrast, glinted ever brighter in the Mozambican sun, where the Shangaan still prosper today.

## HISTORICAL CALENDAR

**2000BC** Nomadic hunter-gatherers inhabit the region.
**200BC–AD300** Bantu tribes displace indigenous people.
**c300** Persian–Arab communities on Ibo/Mozambique islands.
**1497–98** Da Gama lands at Mozambique en route to India.
**1507–15** Portuguese erect a fort on Ilha de Moçambique.
**1510** The rise of the Monomotapa myth.
**1570–1600** Portuguese traders attacked along Zambezi River.
**1709** Portuguese captaincies established at Sena, Tete, Zumbo and Manica.
**1752** Mozambican government is separated from Goa.

Portuguese secretariat on Ilha de Moçambique.
**1781** Huge *prazos* (land leases) granted to Portuguese settlers who then resist Portuguese authority for nearly 150 years.
**1808** Madagascan pirates raid Ibo and Mozambique islands.
**1830** Slave trade between Mozambique/Brazil at a peak.
**1891** Anglo-Portuguese treaty defines colonial borders.
**1933** Mozambique becomes a *de jure* province of Portugal.
**1940–60** Immigration raises settler population to 100,000.
**1960** Frelimo supporters massacred at Mueda.
**1974** Colonial territories ceded by Socialist junta in Portugal.

**1975** Flag of independent Mozambique raised in Maputo.
**1977** Renamo formed by Rhodesian Secret Service.
**1984** Nkomati Accord ends South African support of Renamo troops.
**1992** Renamo and Frelimo sign peace treaty in Rome.
**1994** Frelimo wins elections; Joaquim Chissano is President.
**1998** Second democratic elections, Renamo defeated narrowly and Chissano remains president.
**2000** Huge MOZAL aluminium smelter opens near Maputo.
**2005** Chissano hands over power to Armando Guebuza.

### RISE OF THE MONOMOTAPA

In the history of east-central Africa two names stand out: Great Zimbabwe (centred on the stone citadel at present-day Masvingo in Zimbabwe) and Monomotapa (a grouping of Karanga chieftaincies). In the late 15th century, the decline of Great Zimbabwe, for 1000 years a centre of trade and religion, was paralleled by the rise of the Monomotapa (more properly the *Mwenu Mutapa*). At this time, dominant Zimbabwe families moved north, but ruins at Manyikeni, west of Mapinhane, prove that sections of the Karanga elite moved southeastwards.

## Portuguese Expansion and Local Resistance

By 1550, the Portuguese had wrested the coastal trading monopoly from the Arabs. The coastal forts needed to guard their dominion, however, were disease-ridden, the pay was low, discipline oppressive and Portuguese women a rarity. Men frequently ventured inland to trade firearms, and married the daughters of chiefs just like their Islamic predecessors. These opportunists had no official sanction and were largely ignored by the Portuguese authorities until the murder, in 1561, of Gonçalo da Silveira, a fanatical Castilian missionary bent on the conversion of the Monomotapa. His murder came at a time when Portugal was looking to place more people under its land tax umbrella. In 1571 the Portuguese king sent a consort with presents (never to be delivered) for the Karanga king. Four years later Francisco Barreto left for the Monomotapa gold mines, only to be thwarted by local tribes. In 1573, a second expedition wiped out Muslim traders at Sena and erected earth-walled forts at Tete and Sena. This extension of Portuguese control enabled them to subjugate most of the Karanga chieftaincies by the mid-18th century.

### The *Prazo* Problem

Until they were outlawed in the 1930s, the *prazos de coroa* (leased crown estates) were one of Mozambique's most fascinating features. They were not introduced to deprive indigenous people of their land, but evolved when white rene-

**Above:** *The 16th-century fortress of São Sebastião on Ilha de Moçambique provided refuge for the islanders during raids by Betsimisaraka slavers.*

gades established niches for themselves within African society, often through marriage. The *prazo* communities produced new cultural and social practices reflecting their Afro–Asian–European mix.

The Portuguese crown granted land to religious orders, noblemen and discharged soldiers who often recruited private armies to extract further concessions from local chiefs. By 1670, *muzungo* (Afro-Portuguese) warlords had extorted most of northern **Karangaland** for themselves. Predictably, this lawlessness prevented the development and taxation of the region, thus becoming a major headache for the Portuguese administration. The government offered to recognize land claims on condition that *prazo* holders kept order, maintained roads, provided soldiers and paid for the upkeep of government buildings. In an attempt to increase the number of European women in Mozambique, *prazo* concessions were granted to orphaned girls and widows. Since women were often left widowed several times, some (the famed *Donas*) managed to accumulate vast tracts of land by way of a succession of marriages.

### Slaves, Pirates and the Scramble for Africa

In 1808 a fleet of war canoes appeared along the northern Mozambique coast, the biggest of several assembled by **Betsimisaraka** chiefs from Madagascar between 1800 and 1820, in search of slaves. The

## LOURENÇO MARQUES

Although a Portuguese trader named Lourenço Marques had sailed into this 'Bay of the Lagoon' (now Maputo Bay) in 1544, the site of present-day **Maputo** (formerly Lourenço Marques) consisted of little more than makeshift dwellings around the *Fortaleza da Nossa Senhora da Conceição*. As the safest natural harbour between Cape Town and Ilha de Moçambique, the bay became the focus of British expansion from the south. The resulting territorial dispute between **Britain** and **Portugal** was eventually arbitrarily settled in favour of Portugal by French president, **Marie Edmé MacMahon**. Lourenço Marques developed swiftly, and eventually inherited the status of capital from Ilha de Moçambique.

ferocity of the invaders partially depopulated the coast from Kilwa (Tanzania) to Ilha de Moçambique (Mozambique Island). In 1816 the Afro-Portuguese on Ibo retreated to the protection of the fort and repelled the pirates. These attacks decimated communities which had themselves lived off the slave trade for centuries.

The east African slave trade accelerated when France, expanding sugar plantations on its Indian Ocean possessions, needed extra labour. Despite having banned other European powers from trading on the Mozambican coast, the Portuguese quickly instituted large-scale slaving, receiving foodstuffs and silver in return. By 1775 the French were exporting about 1500 slaves a year from the islands of Ibo and Mozambique. When the Napoleonic Wars disrupted the slave trade between West Africa and America, buyers looked to Mozambique, which exported 30,000 souls in 1828.

In 1875 the Portuguese abolished slavery and *prazos*, attempting to replace them with citizenship, legal rights and the duty to pay taxes and do military service. During the 1884 **Berlin Congress**, Britain contested Portugal's presence in Mozambique, insisting that effective occupation was the only acceptable basis for territorial claims. When **Cecil J Rhodes**' British South Africa Company officially claimed free navigation of the Zambezi, Portugal countered by sending two steam gunships upriver to protect Massingir. The British demanded their retreat and issued orders to mobilize their own fleet. The Portuguese capitulated in January 1890, and although some wrangling followed, Mozambique's borders have changed little since then.

### Greater Autonomy and World War I

Ilha de Moçambique lost its capital status to the southern port of **Lourenço Marques** in 1902 due to the latter's increased economic links with South Africa. Despite Lisbon giving increased autonomy to Mozambique in the 1920s, Portugal-oriented administrators continued to rule the colony, excluding the settlers and Afro-Portuguese from power. During the closing stages of

**World War I** Portugal joined the winning side to secure its colonial possessions. In 1926 a military coup overthrew the government of Portugal and by 1930 a professor of finance, **Antonio Salazar**, began to take control of the country's affairs, creating a closed economic system with the colonies. The **Colonial Act** of 1933 made Mozambique a province of the Portuguese state, with a common law and centrally planned economy.

## From Liberation Struggle to Democracy

After World War II, awakening **African nationalism** began to challenge the colonial powers. Portuguese attempts to isolate Mozambique from this trend were thwarted by returning migrant labourers who had been exposed to liberation politics. **Manu**, an early Mozambican independence movement, gathered in 1960 to petition the Portuguese administrator in Mueda, but troops ended the demonstration by shooting dozens of civilians. Atrocities like this helped to politicize Mozambicans, and **Frelimo** (Mozambican Liberation Front) was formed in Dar es Salaam in 1962. Frelimo's armed wing, the FPLM (Popular Mozambique Liberation Forces), launched its **armed struggle** with an attack on Chai in northern Mozambique on 25 September 1964. Initially, Frelimo's campaign was unsuccessful, but after the assassination of leader Eduardo Mondlane in 1969, new commandant **Samora Machel** mounted attacks as far south as Tete and Manica. Meanwhile the Portuguese had been diverting investment from Mozambique to the EEC (European Economic Community). When the April 1974 revolution brought a new anticolonial regime to power in Portugal, Mozambican soldiers defected, political prisoners were released and the governor general recalled to Lisbon.

**Opposite:** *A statue of Samora Machel, Maputo.* **Below:** *Samora Machel in battle fatigues – a mural near Maputo's airport.*

**Opposite:** *Maputo street scene showing the red-roofed Banco Commercial building.*

Chaos ensued and white settlers fled to **South Africa** in their thousands. On 25 June 1975 Mozambique gained independence, Portugal recognizing the Frelimo government without insisting on elections. Shortly afterwards, almost all skilled administrators and workers departed, leaving behind Frelimo personnel who adopted (often disastrous) policies rooted in Marxist theory rather than on any knowledge of the job at hand.

## Civil War and the New Mozambique

In 1977 the government of **Rhodesia** (now Zimbabwe) secretly formed the rebel **Renamo** (Mozambique National Resistance) movement to destroy transport and communication links. From 1977–92 Mozambique was devastated by banditry and civil war which destroyed the social and economic fabric of the entire nation. During this period Frelimo experienced many difficulties in trying to govern Mozambique. After Zimbabwe's independence in 1980 and its withdrawal of support, South Africa backed Renamo which sought external credibility as an anticommunist movement. In 1984, presidents **Botha** of South Africa and **Machel** of Mozambique signed the **Nkomati Accord**, agreeing not to support armed insurrection in each other's countries. Machel travelled abroad, shunning his Marxist backers by visiting Britain and Portugal, a campaign cut short by the 1986 air crash which tragically ended his life. It was left to Joaquim Chissano to bring Renamo to heel.

At its third congress (1990), in keeping with world trends, Frelimo formally departed from its disastrous **Marxist-Leninist** ideology, while the collapse of the Soviet Union hastened the Russian departure. Renamo rebels continued to sabotage the infrastructure until a **cease-fire** agreement was signed on 15 October 1992. UN-supervised democratic multiparty elections were held in 1994. Mozambique's reconstruction progressed quickly. Truce paved the way for the deployment of a UN peacekeeping force (Onumoz) which facilitated the disarmament of all armed groups. In the face of a sceptical world, Frelimo

### SOVIET MOZAMBIQUE

During the Cold War the former Soviet Union exported its brand of international Marxism to Africa. By 1958 Mozambican guerillas trained by Russian advisers were launching regular raids from Tanzania. In 1974, unexpectedly, a socialist revolution in Portugal toppled the Portuguese government and Mozambique was literally handed over to Frelimo. Not ready to govern, Frelimo persecuted white Mozambicans and they left in droves. Russian advisers arrived to fill the vacuum. Insulating themselves from the locals, their officials pillaged natural resources like wildlife, forests and seafood. By the time the Soviets left, after the collapse of communism in 1991, few Mozambicans lamented although some Russian and Cuban agricultural and veterinary advisors did train local people.

and Renamo laid down arms and began campaigning in the political arena.

Finally, in 1997, the reopening of Gorongosa National Park, formerly Renamo headquarters, as well as peaceful elections in 1999 and 2004, symbolized a peaceful and prosperous new era for the country.

## GOVERNMENT AND ECONOMY
### The New Mozambique

Mozambique must certainly count as one of the success stories of the worldwide UN peacekeeping operations.

South Africa's political transformation, combined with the determination of a people tired of violence, as well as the efforts of aid groups, laid the foundation for Mozambique's highly successful and peaceful November 1994 elections. Today, after the 2004 elections, Frelimo, under Armando Guebuza, may still be the ruling party, but Mozambique is unrecognizable from the days when running water was a luxury, and travellers risked their lives simply by leaving the relative safety of the cities. The government is encouraging development through tourism. Former state-owned enterprises have been privatized, placing them on a sound commercial footing. Freedom of the press is respected (although the 2001 murder of a prominent journalist, Carlos Cardozo, is cause for concern) and local daily newspapers present lively, critical debate on issues of the day.

The combination of a friendly people determined to progress, sound fiscal governance and an exciting natural environment being opened up to visitors, certainly demonstrate that Mozambique has a very positive future indeed.

### TOWERS OF IVORY

Elephant tusks were a much-coveted resource, ruthlessly exploited by the Arabs, the Portuguese and Renamo. 18th- and 19th-century reports speak of boats capsizing under the weight of the tusks while transferring them to bigger ships. Although hunters decimated Mozambique's elephants before sanctuaries such as Gorongosa were proclaimed, it took a civil war to finally silence the great beasts. Mozambique's elephant population was reduced from a proud 20,000 to a few hundred by 1990. Both Renamo rebels and the Frelimo government sold or bartered ivory for weapons. Perhaps it is not surprising that South Africa's 1984 commitment to cease its support of the Renamo movement coincided with the first effective worldwide ban on the ivory trade.

**Right:** *Many containers are lined up in Maputo's busy harbour.*
**Opposite:** *A busy through route – the Nyamapanda border post into Zimbabwe.*

## Economic Reconstruction

For hundreds of years Mozambique was administered from Portugal, and therefore its economic infrastructure was aimed primarily at facilitating the **export** of agricultural, marine, forestry and mineral resources to the mother country. Although Mozambique was still reasonably prosperous in 1975, 95% of the indigenous population was illiterate and only a small handful possessed any formal qualifications or skills.

After the Portuguese withdrew, a transitional government was formed by Frelimo in 1974, and **Joaquim Chissano** took control. The following year **Samora Machel** became leader of Frelimo, and thus the first president of an independent Mozambique, which he declared a one-party Marxist state.

The country's economy slipped into almost total chaos as essential services literally ceased to exist. Soviet and East German troops and advisers were invited by Samora Machel to fill the void. Despite some good intentions, they managed to contribute very little and the economy continued to decline rapidly. In addition, support for Rhodesian and South African liberation movements cost Mozambique dearly and destroyed its last hope for progress.

When President Machel died in a mysterious plane crash in 1986, the country had descended into profound chaos, and it was up to his successor, Joaquim Chissano, to rescue the situation and transform the economy into a **free market system**.

## Rebuilding Mozambique's Roads

Reduced to perilous strips of potholed tarmac by years of neglect and sabotage, Mozambique's roads and bridges have been one of the first of the essential services to receive the government's much-needed attention.

The resurfacing of a strategic 1700km (1056-mile) stretch of the **EN1**, the national road between **Maputo** and **Beira**, has been completed. Despite the floods of 2000 and 2001, most other main routes south of the Zambezi are in satisfactory condition and the strategic link between Beira and Quelimane, via Inchope, Gorongosa and Caia, was completed in 2003. A brand-new toll road on a more direct route between **Ressano Garcia** (Komatipoort in South Africa) and Maputo is now in use. This road is integral to a broad development scheme called the Maputo Corridor.

### PEACE AT LAST

Mozambique today is a nation that has undergone fundamental economic and social transformation. The media are no longer censored and freedom of movement is guaranteed under the new constitution. International investors are supporting huge industrial projects and entrepreneurs are renovating the old lodges and hotels and building new ones. Even in the most remote regions, schools and hospitals have either been rebuilt or are under construction. Buses, trucks and taxis are once more transporting people throughout the country. Since the peace accord of October 1992, Mozambicans have regained a reputation for being among the friendliest in the world.

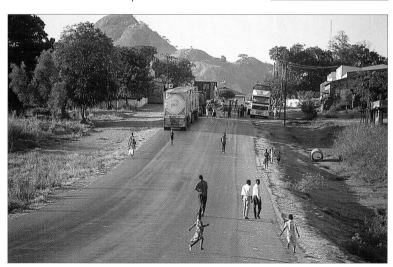

## Agriculture

Prior to 1975, **copra** (dried coconut flesh) formed one of Mozambique's most important exports. In 1979, copra formed 10% of the country's agricultural production. The extracted oils were extensively used by the international cosmetic industry. The main coconut-producing areas are along the coastal plains of the Inhambane, Zambezia and Nampula provinces.

Since coconut plantations are located in coastal areas, copra production is affected by the periodic cyclones that uproot trees and rip unripe fruit from the branches. On the Island of Quirimba north of Pemba, the Gessner family has cultivated coconuts for three generations, and, although cyclone Demoina damaged thousands of trees, their impressive estate of some 40,000 trees was the only one able to function throughout the civil war. Those of us with no use for either copra or coconut husks will be pleased to know that there are other ways to enjoy this delectable fruit. Young green coconuts, known to the locals as *lanhos*, are full of refreshing pure **coconut water**, and are sold on the roadside wherever the palms grow. For a handful of currency, the *lanho* of your choice will have its top lopped off and you will be able to slake the most urgent of thirsts on up to a litre of the delicately sweet fluid – also distilled into a lethal liquor called *sura*.

In 1973, Mozambique exported some 125,000 tonnes of **cashew nuts** – the country's largest food

**Left:** *Fishing is an important source of income for
many Mozambicans.*
**Opposite:** *Cashew nuts
are processed and packed
at this factory in Monapo.*

export at the time. Although by 1983 this amount had
been reduced to a few rotting sackloads, Mozambique
is still the best (and cheapest) country for properly dried
and processed cashew nuts.

### Marine Resources

The occurrence of **prawns** along the Mozambique coast
generally coincides with the location of mangrove
*(mangue)* swamps. The decline of the prawn population, particularly in Maputo Bay, can be ascribed to the destruction
of the mangroves at the Maputo and Incomáti river mouths.
In 1983, the combined catch of commercial and subsistence prawn fishermen was in the region of 10,000 tonnes, the
majority of the prawns originating from the nutrient-rich
waters off Maputo, Sofala and Nampula provinces.

Pelagic fish such as anchovy, barracuda and sardine
are found throughout the shallow coastal waters of the
broad Mozambique Channel. In deeper waters tuna,
marlin and sailfish occur, the St Lazarus Bank east of
Moçímboa da Praia being one of the few places in the
world where marlin are known to breed. Rising long
before dawn, subsistence fishermen still enact an ancient
ritual unifying man and sea as they sail their bamboo
platforms towards the horizon. By mid-morning they
return laden with fish – if the gods have been kind.

Commercial trawlers come from afar to exploit these
riches and this area of the ocean is not exempt from the
worldwide problem of ruthless overfishing.

### AN EMBATTLED ECONOMY

Prior to 1980 Mozambique's
main exports were cashew
nuts, petroleum derivatives,
prawns, tea, sugar and cotton.
The Gross Domestic Product
(GDP) was made up of 50%
agriculture, 40% industry, 5%
transport and communications
with the balance contributed
by commerce and administration. However, such was the
extent of Mozambique's economic decline that, between
1973 and 1983, the country
ceased to be able to feed its
citizens, having to rely on
shipments of foreign food aid
instead. Only the air transport
industry prospered, due to the
frequent ambushes on the
roads and railways. Millions of
Mozambican peasants fled
into neighbouring countries
where they lived in refugee
camps until 1994.

**Right:** *The Cahora Bassa dam fills a beautiful valley.*
**Opposite:** *A woman of the Makua tribe, one of Mozambique's eight main tribal groups.*

### The End of the Work

The name **Cahora Bassa** (Cabora Bassa in colonial times) is probably a corruption of the Chewa term *kebrabassa*, their name for the once magnificent stretch of rapids in the gorge across which the dam was constructed. *Kebrabassa* means 'the end of the work', an appropriate name for the point where traders and travellers, using the Zambezi as a route into the interior, were forced to turn back by the rocks and waterfalls. Boats paddled by locally 'recruited' slaves found their progress blocked at *Kebrabassa* (now Songo), and explorers like David Livingstone, who was searching for a navigable route into central Africa, could only drift back downstream to Tete, probably to the relief of the pitifully treated slaves.

Although Cahora Bassa was a joint venture between South Africa, Portugal and the province of Mozambique, energy transmission along the direct current lines to South Africa was cut in 1986 when **Renamo** rebels sabotaged pylons in response to the termination of their South African support in terms of the **Nkomati Accord**.

Due to sabotage, between 1986 and 1998 no power from Cahora Bassa reached South Africa but a US$150 million programme has rerouted the lines, and a link now provides power direct to the MOZAL aluminium smelter near Maputo. Soon southern Mozambique will no longer rely exclusively on South African electrical utility Eskom for power.

---

**CAHORA BASSA HYDROELECTRIC PROJECT**

- Date of completion: 1974.
- Dam type: double-curved concrete arch.
- Dam height: 160m (525ft).
- Dam wall altitude: 331m (1086ft).
- Length: 270km (168 miles).
- Capacity: 52,000 million $m^3$.
- Average inflow: 2800 cumecs (98,881 cusecs).
- Flood inflow: over 30,000 cubic metres per second.
- Area: 2660$km^2$ (1027 sq miles).
- Catchment area: 1,200,000 $km^2$ (463,200 sq miles).
- Generating potential: 4000 megawatts.
- Length of direct current (DC) transmission lines: (Songo–Apollo near Pretoria), 2400km (1491 miles).
- Length of AC transmission lines: (Songo–Chimoio and Songo–Nampula) 2000km (1243 miles).

# THE PEOPLE

Of the eight major tribal groups resident in Mozambique, the Tsonga (Ronga) dominate the south, the Shona and Zambezi Valley tribes (Chuabo, Sena, Nyungwe) the central region, and the Yao and Makua–Lómwè are dominant in the north.

The 1820 *Mfecane* wars unleashed by Shaka, Zululand's (South Africa) warrior king, generated violent waves of unrest which uprooted hundreds of thousands of people, and reached as far north as Kenya. Small groups of Nguni fled into Mozambique, but scattered on coming into contact with resident tribes to avoid being viewed as a threat. Remnants of the Nguni still cling to the fringes of the Lebombo Mountains near Namaacha, at the confluence of the Limpopo and Shangane rivers, at Espungabera at the headwaters of the Buzi River and on the Angónia Plateau in northern Tete province. Due to its past unsuitability for cattle (tsetse fly was rife), Mozambique was, for the most part, spared destruction by Shaka.

The Makonde tribe of northern Cabo Delgado and southern Tanzania had a reputation for territorial aggression. They had always been staunchly independent, resisting incursions first from the Arabs, and later from the Portuguese. The liberation struggle in Mozambique started with Makonde herders being evicted from their land by Portuguese farmers, a move that was bound to end in bloodshed.

## Language

Of the 17 more important **ethnic languages** spoken in Mozambique, the most common are, in the south: Shangaan, Tswa and Ronga; in the central region: Shona, Sena and Nyanja; the main vernaculars in the north are: Makua, Lómwè, Chuabo, Yao and Makonde and Swahili.

**BASIC SHANGAAN**

Good day • *Absheni*
How are you? • *Minjani?*
I am fine • *Nikhona*
What is this place?
• *Iyini ndawu leyi?*
Where is . . .?
• *Yikwini . . .?*
How much is that?
• *Imalumuni?*
What is your name?
• *Imani bito rawena?*
Thank you • *Nakhensa*
May I take your photograph?
• *Ni nga teka shitombe?*
Where does this road go to?
• *Ndlola loyi yiyakwini?*
What is the name of this in
Shangaan? • *Iyini bito
rashileshi hishi shangaan?*

**Opposite:** *the influence of Arab traders is tangible on Ilha de Moçambique.*
**Below:** *This Catholic church on Ibo Island is said to date back to the 16th century.*

**Portuguese** was and still is the everyday language of commerce and technology – even the Frelimo government declared Portuguese to be the country's official language. A survey undertaken in 1980 revealed that only about 25% of the total urban population could speak Portuguese, with about half this number applicable in the rural areas. Only 10% of Maputo's citizens spoke Portuguese at home, while the proportion of Mozambican citizens who grew up speaking Portuguese was less than 2%. **English** may not easily be understood away from up-market hotels, lodges and restaurants, but don't be surprised if a street urchin in Beira or Maputo suddenly berates you in perfect English for not giving him or her money. Many of Mozambique's children who are under the age of 16 grew up in refugee camps in one of the English-speaking countries surrounding Mozambique. **Funakalo**, the discredited language once spoken mainly by South Africa's black miners, remains a valuable communication medium. However, a few phrases of **Shangaan** will elicit more smiles.

## Religion

During Mozambique's Marxist period, organized religion was suppressed by the Frelimo government, thus no accurate statistics have been kept for this period.

The urbanized population has adopted **Catholicism**, most common in the south, while further north **Islam** becomes more dominant. Traditional practices such as **ancestor worship** and **animism** are still widespread. This was used to profound effect by the protagonists who influenced the Mozambicans both during the period of conflict as well as prior to the first democratic elections in 1994.

## Cultural Heritage

With a coastline settled by adventurers from Arabia, India, China and southern Europe as well as diverse wandering African tribes, Mozambique is a unique mix of cultural practices and beliefs. Although geographically part of southern Africa, this former **Portuguese** colony has a historical and cultural heritage more closely related to **Muslim** northeast Africa, while its population also exhibits a lively, Latin outlook on life.

Whether you enter the country from Malawi, Tanzania (Rovuma crossing by vehicle ferry and dugout at the mouth), Zambia, Zimbabwe, South Africa or Swaziland, by boat via one of the many harbours or by air into Maputo International Airport, you will be faced with the challenge of communicating with people whose command of the **English** language is weak.

Most popular tourist destinations lie along the coast where people live in fishing villages, and dhows are the main means of transport. From meeting places under trees in mud-and-straw 'suburbs' to chic nightclubs in the cities, the music that is belted out everywhere ranges from sensuous **samba**, **salsa** and **rumba** to rowdy **marimba/ timbila** (xylophone) and awesome Afro-Caribbean.

### PASSION IN PEMBA

A night of *enika* (spirit distilled from pineapples), swaying hips and beautiful *mulatto* (mixed race) girls with wild shining eyes, under the palms of Pemba's *bairro* (informal suburb) *Paquete-Quete* is the stirring stuff of a Bob Dylan ballad. Mozambique is an unusual country embracing a cultural mix that resembles a cross between Brazil, India, Arabia and Africa, a contrast to the surrounding English-speaking African states. By Western standards, Mozambique remains desperately poor – yet its people are proud, courteous and very mindful of good manners.

**Right:** *Murals, like this one in Tete, often commemorate the liberation struggle.*
**Opposite:** *Many tourists come to lovely Benguerra Island to fly-fish.*

## Mozambique's Art World

In the 1950s some of the European painters belonging to Lourenço Marque's art nucleus began to feel the challenging burden of living on a continent rich in unrecognized indigenous art forms. Moving away from Eurocentrism, they started addressing local social themes, using visual motifs observed in popular tradition to create works more identifiably 'Mozambican'. Today, big beaming round faces and large white eyes are evidently the way Mozambicans see themselves when painting murals.

By independence in 1975, the liberation movements began to promote local culture. A cultural centre was formed to nurture local art. Most new artists initially imitated the leading figures in Mozambique's plastic arts community. During the 1975–85 period, due to civil turmoil, their imagery dealt mainly with the immediacy of political militancy.

The Mozambican artists' geographical isolation, lack of training and the absence of a formal art trade had an unexpected consequence: a large number of painters were able to make a living by personally marketing and selling their own work. Without the discipline and attention to style demanded by classical art academies, a freshness of style and lack of inhibition was preserved in Mozambique, characteristic of what may be termed the 'Mozambican school'.

## Theatre

Maputo's Teatro Avenida on Avenida 25 de Setembro sometimes hosts stage productions. Mozambique's **Companhia Nacional de Canto e Dança**, based in the Rua de Bagamoio (opposite Luso), also occasionally has shows depicting various traditional dance styles. See the daily newspaper, *Noticias*, and the weekly *Savanna* and www.cncd.org.mz for their programme.

## Sport and Recreation

Mozambique's most popular sports are **basketball**, **soccer** (football) and **athletics**. Maputo's **Maria Mutola** holds the world record and won the gold medal in Paris during 2003 for the women's 800m indoor track race. Basketball has thrived and the national team has been African champion for years. Most of the main cities and towns have indoor basketball courts, with the club in steamy Quelimane being particularly competitive. Golfers can only play in Maputo, where the accepted obstacles at the **Campo de Golfe de Maputo**, a little inland from Costa do Sol, are fairways lined with tin shanties, and people doing their laundry in the water hazards. The local population of Morrungulo is threatening to install a few greens among the palms and dunes.

---

### ART AND ARCHITECTURE

**Makonde:** in a remote area straddling the Mozambique/Tanzania border, the Makonde tribe's sculptures depict a bizarre mixture of ancestor worship and Christianity.

**Malangatana:** this celebrated painter used disturbing surreal images of violence to publicise the horrors of war.

**Manueline:** ornate style of architecture popular during the reign of King Emanuel I of Portugal. He transformed Portugal into a maritime power and his reign is considered to be the most brilliant in the country's history. The **Natural History Museum** in Maputo was built in the Manueline/neo-Gothic style.

**Art Deco:** characterized by geometrical shapes. Maputo has some fine examples of this style along the Avenida Samora Machel.

### PREPARE A CHUABO DISH

You need: a bowl of Nyemba (red beans) or manioc (cassava) leaves (spinach will do equally well); a clove of garlic; chopped piri-piri; pinch of salt; coconut water (inside the nut); coconut milk (obtained by squeezing the flesh of the nut); and maybe a handful of ground cashew nuts and some fresh prawns. Crush leaves with the garlic, piri-piri and salt. Boil until soft. Add the water and milk from the coconut and add cashew nuts and prawns. Cook for 10 minutes over moderate heat and serve hot.

## Food and Drink

A continental characteristic which has remained firmly entrenched in the larger Mozambican towns such as Maputo, Beira and Quelimane is the love of wine, company and song. The Portuguese standard here is: *entradas* (entrées) of *prego* (steak roll), *chouriço* (spicy sausage), *rissois* (shrimps in batter) and *sopa de mariscos* (shellfish soup) followed by a main dish of perhaps *lulas grelhado* (grilled calamari), *espetada* (kebab), *galinha inteiro com piri-piri* (whole chicken piri-piri), *peixe cozido com todos* (boiled fish, usually cod, with rice or potato chips, and tomato salad) or perhaps *caranguejo recheado* (stuffed crab). Top it all with a *pudim* (pudding) of *gelado sorvete* (ice cream sorbet) and *salada de frutas* (fruit salad).

Since Mozambique's climate ranges from tropical to temperate and from arid to very humid, indigenous and cultivated fruit and vegetables available are rich

in variety. Rainfall, generally speaking, increases from south to north, decreasing from east to west, and so does the availability and assortment of food. Fresh Portuguese-style bread rolls (*pãozinho*), often baked in hollowed-out ant hills (*termitária*), are widely available throughout the country, even in the most isolated places. As long as you have something to smear on that hot loaf (*pão*), you need never go hungry.

To savour the delicious assortment of Mozambican fruit and vegetables at its best, it is necessary to take the effect of seasonal influences into account. Nicoadala near Quelimane may produce some of the world's largest, juiciest and sweetest **pineapples**, while the **papaya** at Pemba is surely worth the airfare on LAM from Maputo. But if you arrive in August

**Left:** *A Chimoio woman, her baby tied securely on her back, sifts maize meal.*
**Opposite:** *A barbecue on Magaruque Island consists of delicious crayfish tails.*

(winter in Mozambique), both these delicious crops will be in extreme short supply and you will have to settle for bananas, tomatoes and green vegetables. Of course, along the coast there is always **seafood**, while inland the staple diet is *mandioca* (**cassava**) and *sima* (**corn porridge**).

If you are cooking for yourself and intend shopping at the markets, carry a small fisherman's scale, as well as your own selection of condiments and herbs. Even if you intend eating out, some restaurants do not offer a decent selection of condiments, so it is always wise to carry salt and pepper cellars, lemon juice and whatever sauces you can't live without.

Note that the **service** in rural restaurants (where it exists at all) is usually painfully **slow**, almost comically so. Your well-meaning waiter may consider two hours a reasonable preparation time for your meal, and would feel mortally insulted by complaints about the delay, or the cold food.

## MOZAMBICAN DELIGHTS

**Matata** (shrimp and peanut stew) is a typical local main-stay. Imagine a combination of shrimps, peanuts, crushed coconut and tender, young spinach. Chopped red pepper is optional.

**Frango a Cafriál** (barbecued chicken) is a plump chicken rubbed down with hot piri-piri sauce and roasted over an open charcoal brazier.

**Sopa de Feijão Verde** (green bean soup) has fresh green beans cut across in thin slices, boiled and served in a thin tomato and onion purée.

**Salada de Pera Abacate** (avocado salad) is served on a bed of crisp lettuce, doused with a herb, olive oil and lemon dressing.

**Ananas con Vinho do Porto** (fresh pineapple in port): a little sugar, some crushed, roasted cashew nuts and, of course, a helping of port, lib-erally sprinkled on the fruit.

# 2
# Maputo

This important southern Indian Ocean port lies less than 100km (60 miles) from neighbouring Swaziland and South Africa. With its subtropical climate, beautiful sheltered bay and blend of Portuguese architecture, African spontaneity and Indo/Portuguese/African cuisine, Maputo (formerly Lourenço Marques) has retained much of its colonial mystique. Nightclubs swing to samba rhythms until dawn and a host of *quiosques* (kiosks) serve *galinha piri-piri* (chicken piri-piri), *matapas* (a cassava-leaf dish), *bacalhau* (dried cod) and some of the best *batatas frita* (fried potato chips) in the world. Hundreds of *salões* (sidewalk cafés), dozens of nightclubs and the odd sleazy strip joint complement the vibrant atmosphere of this capital city that feels more Latin American than African.

Modelled on Portuguese harbour cities such as Lisbon and Porto, Maputo's wide *avenidas* (avenues) are lined with pavements inlaid with black-and-white stone mosaics. Laid out in a grid pattern in 1847, the 'long' avenues extend at right angles to **Avenida da Marginal** while the 'short' avenues traverse Maputo Hill away from the bay. By car, you will enter the city via the large traffic circle on Av. 24 de Julho, and proceed for 5km (3 miles) before reaching Av. Julius Nyerere, the heart of the *cima*, or upper city. Visitors arriving at **Maputo International Airport** will enter the city via Av. de Acordos de Lusaka. This becomes Av. da Guerra Popular on reaching the high-rise area, runs downhill to the *baixa* – the lower city – and ends at the massive 'peace goddess' statue in the centre of the square opposite the Maputo Railway Station.

## Don't Miss

*** **Feira Popular:** funfair complex with over 30 pubs restaurants and nightclubs.
** **Mercado Xipamanine:** notorious and exotic market in Mafalala, where you really *can* buy anything.
** **Av. da Marginal:** walk along the promenade where vendors exhibit their wares.
* **Catembe:** take a ferry across the bay for a wonderful view of the Maputo skyline.
* **Kowhana:** join the locals at this nightclub in Mafalala and lambada until dawn.

**Opposite:** *Aerial view over Maputo's Jardim Tunduru Botanical Gardens.*

## THE STREETS OF MAPUTO

As in most poor, third-world cities, parts of Maputo are home to the destitute and homeless. Street children are always on hand to guard your car or help you with parking. Yet a daylight stroll through the city centre will reveal sights ranging from tailored trees in **Jardim Tunduru Botanical Gardens** to the elegance of the **Hotel Polana**. Downtown Maputo's central market is clearly not a place to flash your wallet or video camera. Here the elite and the public mingle, as they haggle over tobacco, traditional medicine, papaya and prawns.

## CHIEF MAPUTA'S CAPITAL

When the first Portuguese explorers landed on this coast over 500 years ago, they came into contact with an indigenous people ruled by Chief Maputa. Consequently, the area from Maputo Bay south to Lake St Lucia in South Africa's KwaZulu-Natal province was, and still is, often referred to as **Maputaland**. Mozambique's original capital for 200 years was the town of Mozambique, on a little island (now called Ilha de Moçambique/Mozambique Island) about 1500km (932 miles) northeast from Maputo. The Portuguese virtually ignored their little fortified settlement at Delagoa Bay (now Maputo Bay) until the British and the Boers began to show serious interest in the area. The MacMahon Award of 1873 eventually resolved the territorial dispute in Portugal's favour, resulting in a swiftly developing settlement. The Portuguese named it **Lourenço Marques** (now Maputo) and it inherited the status of capital from Ilha de Moçambique in 1897.

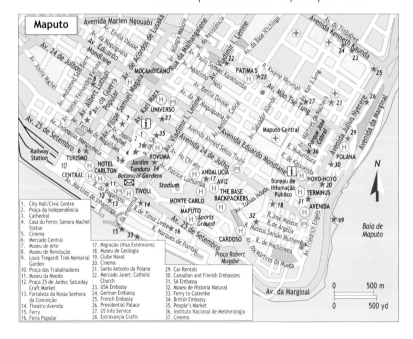

Maputo

1. City Hall/Civic Centre
2. Praça da Independência
3. Cathedral
4. Casa de Ferro; Samora Machel Statue
5. Cinema
6. Mercado Central
7. Museu de Arte
8. Museu de Revolução
9. Louis Tregardt Trek Memorial Garden
10. Praça dos Trabalhadores
11. Museu da Moeda
12. Praça 25 de Junho; Saturday Craft Market
13. Fortaleza de Nossa Senhora da Conceição
14. Theatro Avenida
15. Ferry
16. Feira Popular

17. Migração (Visa Extensions)
18. Museu de Geologia
19. Clube Naval
20. Cinema
21. Santo Antonio da Polana
22. Mercado Janet; Catholic Church
23. USA Embassy
24. German Embassy
25. French Embassy
26. Presidential Palace
27. US Info Service
28. Extravância Crafts

29. Car Rentals
30. Canadian and Finnish Embassies
31. SA Embassy
32. Museu de Historia Natural
33. Ferry to Catembe
34. British Embassy
35. People's Market
36. Instituto Nacional de Metéorologia
37. Cinema

0      500 m

0      500 yd

## Fortaleza da Nossa Senhora da Conceição *

This squat red-sandstone fortress, built between 1851 and 1867, stands on the site of the original mud-and-pole stockade. Once a museum glorifying Portugal's colonial conquests, it is now the **State Historical Archive** and houses the remains of **Ngungunhane**, last great chief of the **Nguni** tribe, who ruled the Gaza region until British and Portuguese expansion led to friction. He was captured and paraded through the streets of Lisbon before dying in exile in the Azores.

## Historic City Sites **

On the bay of Maputo, which is in fact drained mangrove swampland, many colonial buildings still stand along the **Rua do Bagamoio**. There is the **Hotel Central** and the restored **Hotel Carlton**. The **Museu da Moeda** (Currency Museum) near the end of Rua do Bagamoio is Maputo's oldest intact example of Moorish architecture and has been beautifully restored to its original state. Open Tuesday to Thursday, and Saturday.

In an attempt to escape the mosquitoes and humidity of the bay, Maputo's first hospital was erected on an (originally) densely forested hill, in an area that is now characterized by high-rise residential developments. The attractive two-storey Victorian **Central Hospital** has since been converted and is today known as **Restaurante 1908**. The city's hospital moved to larger premises next door.

**Above:** *Maputo's skyline as seen from the harbour.*
**Below:** *This wall motif in the Hotel Central displays a group of musicians.*

## MAPUTO'S MAGICAL MARKETS

• **Mercado Central:** On Av. 25 de Setembro; in existence for over 100 years. Frozen fish, Nampula cashews, Inhambane baskets; mind your pockets.
• **Mercado Xipamanine:** In the heart of Mafalala district. Get a local to take you to see the bizarre array of traditional medicines.
• **Bazar Artesanato:** Toys sold on the Praça 25 de Junho every Saturday. Makonde sculptures available.
• **Mercado Janet:** End Av. Mao Tse Tung. Best selection of local fruit and vegetables.
• **Bazar do Peixe (Fish market):** Opposite the abandoned hotel on Av. da Marginal on the way to Costa do Sol. Watch out for a few fresh prawns placed on top of the rotten ones underneath.

## HISTORICAL AND CULTURAL WALKS

Despite Maputo's reputation for being riddled with thieves and muggers, it is fairly safe to see the sights on foot as long as you carry your passport (or locally notarized copy), leave your valuables behind, walk in a group and return well **before sunset**. Strolling certainly beats the frustration of trying to find parking in a city where windshields, headlamps and indicator lenses are stolen, to the extent that many owners deliberately crack these in an attempt to eliminate their resale value.

To escape the sticky midday heat, the best time to walk is during the **early morning**, especially on **Saturdays** and **Sundays**. 'Maputenses' seem superstitious about exposure to the early morning sun, and so traffic should be light till around 10:00, with another quiet spell during the afternoon siesta (religiously adhered to from 12:00–14:00). Since the two routes allow many opportunities to slake your thirst with tea, coffee, sodas or something sturdier, it's unnecessary to carry anything with you except money and maybe some toilet paper. Those who experience anxiety attacks at the thought of dirty toilets, fear not: clean ablutions are all part of the recommended two routes, which are both circular, not longer than 8km (5 miles) and have safe parking at the point of departure and return (still, don't leave valuables in your vehicle).

### Baixa Walk (lower city): 8km; 5 miles ★★

Starting and finishing on the **Rua da Sé** at the Hotel Rovuma (which has been completely renovated), this route takes in historic old Maputo, and includes a very cheap (if on foot) government ferry ride (the terminal is a 15-minute walk from the hotel) across the bay and back. The hotel is situated opposite the huge, white **Catholic Cathedral** of **Nossa Senhora da Conceição** off Praça da Independência. If you get lost, look for the towering, white spire of the cathedral, which is one of the city's most unmistakable landmarks.

Stand with your back to the hotel lobby, turn right and walk a short distance uphill to Av.

Ho Chi Min. Now swing left (around the back of the cathedral) to the rear of the **City Hall** and **Civic Centre** (Conselho Municipal), which was completed in 1945. For permission to enter the Civic Centre, ask at the reception off Av. Ho Chi Min.

From the front (bay side) of the City Hall, walk down the stairs to the Praça da Independência, and turn right

off the square onto Av. Josina Machel, named after Mozambique's former First Lady. Four blocks further (on the LHS) lies the meticulously maintained **Tregardt Trek Memorial Garden** which commemorates the disastrous attempts by the Transvaal Boers to secure a seaport at the end of the 19th century. The incredible journey of the pioneers is depicted in relief on marble mosaic maps on the boundary walls, as well as on the floor of the pond.

From the monument retrace your steps along Av. Josina Machel to the circle, cross to the newly restored, original LM Club (now the **French Cultural Centre**) and walk up to **Casa do Ferro** designed by French engineer Alexandre Eiffel (*see* p. 39). Across from this prefabricated steel edifice stands the imposing statue of Samora Machel, to the side of which is the entrance to the peaceful **Jardim Tunduru Botanical Gardens**.

You are now on the wide avenue named after Samora Machel, which runs uphill from the *baixa* to the City Hall. Continue downhill to Av. 25 de Setembro (referring to the first day of the revolution) with its high-rise office blocks and shady sidewalk cafés like the **Scala** or **Café Continental**. Turn right at this intersection and continue for two blocks to the **Mercado Municipal** on your right. The market offers a maze of stalls that carry anything from fresh and frozen seafood, colourful tropical fruit and odorous traditional medicines to handicraft, cloth, curios and spices. Watch out for con artists and pickpockets.

**Above:** *The Louis Tregardt Trek Memorial Garden commemorates the Boer pioneers' perilous journey into Mozambique.*
**Opposite:** *The beautiful Catedral de Nossa Senhora da Conceição in Maputo.*

---

**ECHOES OF PAST GRANDEUR**

Already majestic from the outside, it is the interior of the neoclassical **Civic Centre** that is really rewarding. There are magnificent crystal chandeliers, intricate tile mosaics of Portuguese ships, Louis XIV fittings and furniture. Beside the marble staircase in the reception hall are beautiful scale models of the historic buildings of old Maputo.

Leave the **Mercado Municipal** via its main entrance and cross Av. 25 de Setembro to the Rua da Mesquita. Now walk towards the docks and you will pass Maputo's first **mosque** on your left, before reaching an unmistakable landmark, the Victorian **Hotel Central** on the corner of Mesquita and Bagamoio streets. You are now right in the heart of the *baixa,* or downtown Maputo. A right turn takes you to Maputo Station.

New York may have its Lady Liberty, but Praça dos Trabalhadores could hold a candle to it anytime. An intimidating 10m (33ft) stone statue of the Greek goddess Athena, sculpted from Portuguese granite after World War I by Rui Gameiro, is represented staring sternly towards the entrance of the railway station, sword and shield in hand. Local legend tells of a formidable woman who rid the area of a fearsome snake by boiling it in a pot of water balanced on her head.

Almost 90 years after it was constructed, Maputo's **CFM Railway Station** (*Caminhos de Ferro de Moçambique*) looks grubby though extensive renovations were completed in 1997. From the station, return to Hotel Central and carry on down Rua do Bagamoio past the Dance Academy on your right and the Luso nightclub on your left, towards the leafy Praça 25 de Junho (a square named in honour of Mozambique's Day of Independence). One street before the Praça you will see the big and opulent **Cinema 333**. The **Museu da Moeda** and the **Fortaleza da Nossa Senhora da Conceição** (1781) gird the Praça 25 de Junho, which hosts a wonderful craft market (**Bazar Artesanato**) on Saturday mornings. Once the museum of military history, the fortress is now being transformed into the State Historical Archive. Open 07:00–17:00 weekends only.

## TRANQUIL TROPICAL GARDENS

Laid out in 1883 by English landscaper Thomas Honney, who created similar parks for the King of Greece and the Sultan of Turkey, Maputo's **Jardim Tunduru Botanical Gardens** today offer a splendid escape from the bustle of the city. Hundreds of colourful shrubs, hedges and flowering plants are shaded by towering indigenous and exotic trees. The murmur of streams and the splash of fountains complement the feeling of peace. Don't miss out on a visit to the conservatory (obtain permission at the nearby office) filled with cycads, ferns and conifers, among which statues of water nymphs hide.

From the fort, stroll along Av. Mártires de Inhaminga, which runs parallel to the docks, past an open field on the left to the new **Ministry of Finance** building. Here, turn towards the bay and board the rusty **ferry** at the jetty opposite the corner of Rua da Imprensa and Av. 10 de Novembro. The ferry will take you across **Maputo Bay** to the suburb of **Catembe**, a 15-minute journey costing the price of a loaf of bread. The service begins at 06:00 and ends at 20:00, with departures approximately every hour. Vehicles can be transported at a charge of around US$20.

In Catembe you could have lunch at the **Restaurante Marisol** in the delightful Catembe Gallery Hotel, a 20-minute walk left from the ferry terminal. The hotel has a pool, shady gardens and great views of Maputo's skyline.

After taking the ferry back to Maputo, turn right along Av. 10 de Novembro which runs along the bay. After a few hundred metres turn left into Rua António Fernandes (Complexo Zambi is on the corner) and one block up walk left into the **Feira Popular** complex. Wander among the pubs, clubs and funfair rides (open in the evenings) and exit away from the bay onto Av. 25 de Setembro. Turn left and make your way back towards the central market. After a block turn right into Av. Vladimir Lenine, on the corner of which stands a 33-storey building. Climb the stairs (lifts are often out of order) to the top if you are still energetic enough and wish to see the **best views of Maputo**. There is refreshment at **Café Ma Stop** and international public phones on the ground floor. One block up on Av. Vladimir Lenine, keep to your left to enter the **Jardim Tunduru Botanical Gardens** and take the diagonal path up to Av. Patrice Lumumba. Diagonally opposite the former **LM Radio Station** (now Radio Moçambique Studio), the British embassy was the first in the country and is still housed in the beautiful building. Turn left, then right, back up to Hotel Rovuma for a well-deserved pot of tea.

> ### FEIRA POPULAR
>
> Known to the locals simply as 'Feira', this fairground is an authentic Mozambican place to party the night away. Although rides operate only over weekends, the numerous pubs, clubs, kiosks and restaurants are open nightly. They range from reasonably priced Portuguese family restaurants like quaint **O'Coquero** to **O'Escorpião**, one of the city's most popular restaurants.

**Opposite:** *One of the many shops in Maputo's Municipal (or Central) Market.*
**Below:** *The mural at the former LM Radio Station, now Radio Mozambique.*

## MAPUTO'S MUSEUMS

**Museu de Revolução:**
At 3003 Av. 24 de Julho.
Mainly exhibits of **historical
interest**; emphasis on the
struggle for independence.
**Museu de Geologia:** On
Av. 24 de Julho. Interesting
Manueline architecture;
collection of **precious
stones and minerals**.
**Museu da Moeda:** On Praça
de 25 de Junho, opposite the
Banco de Mozambique. Oldest
intact building in Maputo;
houses **currency** and **barter
items** from around the world.
**Museu de Arte:** On Av. Ho
Chi Min. Displays of local
**paintings** and **sculptures**.

**Opposite:** *This building
in Maputo houses the
Natural History Museum.*
**Below:** *The elegant lobby
of the Hotel Polana exudes
luxury and refinement.*

## Cima Walk (uptown): 7km; 4 miles ★★★

This walk, starting and ending at the **Hotel Polana**
(designed by renowned British architect Sir Herbert
Baker), explores the newer part of Maputo. Built on a
hill overlooking the bay, the Polana, where there is safe
short-term parking, recalls the opulent 1920s when no
expense was spared on style and luxury. It is a fascinating place to visit. The Polana's marvellous lift, with
its carved hardwood panels, ornate iron railings and
crystal windows, is on its own worth the trip.

Walk out of the Polana parking area, cross over Av.
Julius Nyerere, turn right then, after crossing Av. Mao Tsé
Tung, on your left you'll see two stately old colonial
homes. The first villa is still occupied by the descendants
of the original owners, while the second was the **Ungumi
Restaurant**, once the finest dining establishment in town.

From here, continue around the building onto the
Rua Kwame Nkrumah. To the right, one block up from
here is the **Church of Santo António da Polana**. Do
enter this serene building and admire the enormous
stained-glass windows extending into the soaring spire.

One block further on, take a left turn into Av.
Mártires da Machava. After five blocks you will reach
Av. Eduardo Mondlane with its four traffic lanes. On a
corner to your left, is the Bureau de Informação Público
(**Public Information Bureau**, also known as BIP), on
the ground floor of
the meteorological
institute, which offers
a good variety of
useful and informa-
tive videos, books
and magazines about
Mozambique.

From here, turn to
the right and proceed
along Av. Eduardo
Mondlane, past the
sprawling grounds of
the **Central Hospital**

to the lovely and unmistakable **Restaurante 1908**. This elegant Victorian-style mansion, which was once the hospital of Lourenço Marques (Maputo's pre-independence name), has been converted into a restaurant that serves a variety of very good Italian dishes.

Cross Av. Eduardo Mondlane to Av. Salvador Allende and walk four blocks towards the bay. At the junction with Av. Patrice Lumumba turn left and enjoy the excellent view during the short walk to the **Natural History Museum**, built in the Manueline/neo-Gothic style. Exhibits include stuffed animals and the only known collection of elephant foetuses, displaying most of the 22 months of gestation. The museum director, Dr Augusto Cabral, has a wry sense of humour and is a fount of information on Mozambique's history and wildlife.

Walk back around the praça and turn left into Rua de Mateus Sansão Muthemba with **Clube dos Empresários** almost immediately to your left. The shady terrace overlooking the swimming pool is a great place to sit and sip a cold drink. Carry on down the road, watching out for the Associação Cultural Tchova Xitaduma on your right, two blocks before the intersection with Av. Julius Nyerere. This cultural centre often has exhibitions and music produced by local artists.

Continue with Sansão Muthemba and turn left at the junction into Av. Julius Nyerere, on which the Hotel Polana is situated. It is now a 2km (1¼-mile) walk back to your starting point, along a leafy avenue lined with stately homes, interesting shops and many and various restaurants. Pause for an ice cream, stop off for lunch, watch the passing show over a cup of espresso, and support the curio sellers who offer their art and craft underneath the trees opposite the parking area of the Hotel Polana.

### EIFFEL'S 'HOUSE OF STEEL'

Paris may have its Eiffel Tower, but Alexandre Gustave Eiffel's fame is not restricted to France. Born in Dijon in 1832, he first suggested the use of steel braces and girders to support the 485m (1600ft) Garonne bridge. This innovation was of good use to the sculptor Bartholdi, whose Statue of Liberty would otherwise probably not have been able to withstand the gales in New York Bay. Another of Eiffel's prefabricated steel structures was bolted together to form a two-storey house. The **Casa do Ferro**, next to the Jardim Tunduru Botanical Gardens, was to be the residence of Mozambique's governor general during 1892. However, the building proved too hot for habitation as it wasn't insulated. Today it houses the Department of Museums.

**Above:** *Traditional fishermen along the Incomáti River near Marracuene.*

## AROUND MAPUTO
### Mercado Xipamanine ★★

The history of the Xipamanine market goes back to the days of Lourenço Marques and before, when black traders throughout Mozambique were restricted to the outskirts of cities. Tourists did, however, patronize Xipamanine, which had (and still has) the reputation of selling anything from live leopards to human body parts.

Not much has changed, but today you won't find living, wild creatures apart from the odd pet baboon. To get to Xipamanine, either take a *chapa* (minibus taxi) or, if driving, from Av. Julius Nyerere turn into Av. Eduardo Mondlane and, after 3km (1.8 miles), at the ninth major intersection turn right into Av. de Zâmbia up to Praça 21 de Outubro, and then immediately left into Rua dos Irmãos Roby. Carry on till you arrive at the hectic, mostly open-air marketplace. Ensure that you leave someone to look after your car, or at least don't leave anything of value inside. Guard against pickpockets and bag-snatchers, and be sure to visit the section selling traditional medicines and talismans, where you may gain an insight into the hidden spiritual world of the Shangaan and Ronga tribes.

### Xefina Grande Island ★★

At the end of the Marginal, a short distance out to sea, lie the larger of the two islands which guard the mouth of the Incomáti River. Although a few traditional fishermen inhabit Xefina Grande, the lack of fresh water has prevented extensive settlement, leaving the environment largely unspoiled. Arrange a cruise to the island through Ika Mar, based at the Hotel Cardoso. The island's **beaches** and **snorkelling** offshore are excellent. Alternatively you could explore the tumbledown ruins of the mid-16th-century Portuguese fort and a World War II bunker.

---

### CAFÉ SOCIETY

In Maputo, as in the cities of Portugal, most businesses are closed from 12:00–14:00, some until 15:00, and many don't bother to open at all in the afternoon. Citizens while away this **siesta** period sipping espresso in the shade of one of the city's flamboyant trees (it is often too hot and humid to do anything more energetic anyway). Av. 25 de Setembro boasts quaint cafés, such as the **Continental**, Av. 24 de Julho has **Cristal**, while Av. Julius Nyerere offers **Nautilus** and **Café Maputo**.

## Av. da Marginal ★★★

Maputo's **Marginal** (beach promenade) extends for 10km (6 miles) from the end of Av. 25 de Setembro to the fishing village a short distance past Restaurante Costa do Sol.

Identification firmly in pocket, it is best to begin your promenade at the ferry jetty on Av. 10 de Novembro. Walk towards the bay mouth, passing the **Escola Nautica** (Naval School), after which you will join the Marginal, and the city's *Zona Verde* (green belt – note muggings do occur here), at the large traffic circle. Continue under the flyover and on around the bend to the **Clube Naval** (yacht club), which was built in 1913. The club's pub, restaurant and swimming pool are open to visitors on payment of a temporary membership fee. Next is **Artedif**, a workshop for disabled artisans, in thatched rondavels in the centre of the Marginal. Here a range of curios and leatherwork is on sale and repairs to shoes and bags are also undertaken.

You will pass the Holiday Inn and then find reed furniture, wood carvings and colourful pottery on sale under flamboyant trees. After this, an open but soon-to-be-defunct camp site (caravan park), extends for about 1km (½ mile). Pubs, clubs, *quiosques* and youngsters selling ice-cold beverages from polystyrene boxes line the road all the way to **Restaurante Costa do Sol.** Have lunch at the Bazar do Peixe next to the skeleton of an abandoned hotel, and catch a 'chapa' taxi back to your hotel.

**Below:** *Lovely traditional arts and crafts are for sale along the Avenida da Marginal.*

## Maputo at a Glance

Maputo has a subtropical climate. May–August are driest and coolest – top temperatures around 27°C (68°F); monthly rainfall less than 30mm (1in). October and November are the hottest (up to 35°C). December and January are the wettest, with average monthly rainfall of 150mm (6in).

**Note that the Maputo dialling code is 21.**
**By air:** Flights from Paris, Lisbon, Dar es Salaam, Johannesburg, Durban, Harare, Manzini and Mozambique's provincial capitals (except Inhambane and Chimoio) use **Maputo International Airport**, tel: 46-5074. The **Mozambican airline, LAM** (Linhas Aéreas de Moçambique) has regular domestic flights; tel: 42-6001, fax: 46-5134, www.lam.co.mz/uk-home
**By car:** From South Africa via the new N4 Komatipoort (Lebombo)/Ressano Garcia Toll Road; or from Swaziland via the good-condition Lomahasha/Namaacha route.
**By bus:** Luxury buses do the trip between Maputo and Johannesburg/Pretoria every day. Intercape: www.inter cape.co.za tel: 43-1006, Pretoria tel: (+27 12) 654-4114, and Greyhound: www.greyhound.co.za tel: South Africa 083 915 9000 is the booking hotline.

Maputo International Airport is served by city taxis. Hotel Polana meets all international flights while travel agents will transfer you to other hotels by prior arrangement. Locals use *chapas*, from minibuses to Land Rovers and trucks.
**Car hire:** Avis, www.avis.co.za/main.asp?id=508 tel: 46-5497, fax: 46-4498.
Europcar, www.europcar.com europnr@virconn.com airport tel: 46-6182 , Polana tel: 49-7338/9, fax: 49-7334.
**Imperial** Car Rental, tel: 49-3545, airport tel: 46-5250.
**Air charter companies:** Trans Airways (Maputo to Inhaca return), tel: 46-5108; STA: 49-1765 or 49-2022, Mex: 46-6008, mobile: 82 304477, mex@mex.co.za
www.mex.co.za
**Buses** (long distance):
**Transportes Oliveiras**, terminus at the end of Av. 24 de Julho, tel: 73-2108. **Transportes Virginias** (to Beira), based at Hotel Universo, tel: 42-2225 or 42-7003.
**By train:** The **Komati Train** departs Johannesburg daily for Komatipoort; then *chapa* to Maputo from Ressano Garcia. South Africa toll-free: 086-000-8888, www.spoornet.co.za

### Cima (Uptown)
*LUXURY*
**Hotel Polana and Casino**, 1380 Av. Julius Nyerere, tel: 49-1001/7, fax: 49-1480, www.polana-hotel.com res@polana-hotel.com Stunning views, pool in tropical garden.

**Hotel Cardoso**, 707 Av. dos Mártires de Mueda, tel: 49-1071/5, fax: 49-4054. Splendid sunset views over Maputo Bay.
**Holiday Inn**, Av. da Marginal, tel: 49-5050, fax: 49-7700, himaputo@southernsun.com Near sea, water sports; friendly.
**Hotel Avenida**, 627 Av. Julius Nyerere, tel: 49-2000, www.hotelavenida.co.mz h.avenida@teledata.mz

*MID-RANGE*
**Terminus**, 587 Av. Francisco Orlando Magumbwe, tel: 49-1305/6, fax: 49-1284, term hot@terminus-hotel.com Air conditioned, satellite cable TV.
**Residencial Hoyo-Hoyo**, 837 Av. Francisco Orlando Magumbwe, tel: 49-0701, fax: 49-0724, promotur@zebra.uem.mz Good value. Recommended.
**Hotel Moçambicano**, 961 Av. Filipe Samuel Magaia, tel: 31-0600, fax: 32-3124, mozhotel@isl.co.mz Pool, bar restaurant, air conditioned.
**Costa do Sol**, end of Marginal, tel: 45-0115, fax: 45-0162, res@teledata.mz On the beach, good restaurant.

*BUDGET* (cheapest first)
**The Base Backpackers**, 545 Av. Patrice Lumumba, tel/fax: 30-2723, frannypf@yahoo.com
**Fatima's**, 1317 Av. Mao Tsé Tung near Mercado Janet, tel: 30-3345, fax: 49-4462, fatima@virconn.com www.mozambiquebackpackers.com
**Mozaika Guest House**, 169 Av. Agostinho Neto, Maputo,

## Maputo at a Glance

tel: 30-3939, fax: 30-3956, mozaika_guesthouse@ hotmail.com Air conditioning, pool.

### WHERE TO EAT

**Manjar dos Deuses** (Delicacies of the Gods), 162 Av. Julius Nyerere, tel: 49-6834. Book ahead – closed Saturdays.
**Hotel Polana** (see Where to Stay), tel: 49-1003. Three restaurants offering excellent service, elegance and variety.
**Restaurante Marisol**, Catembe Gallery Hotel, Catembe, tel: 38-0050, fax: 38-0003, office@catembe.net Seafood and traditional.
**Restaurante 1908**, 946 Av. Eduardo Mondlane, Maputo, tel: 42-4834. Mozambican, Italian and Indian.
**Costa do Sol**, tel: 45-5115, fax: 45-5162. Delicious seafood and a garlic-laden Greek salad.
**Mira Doce**, tel: 49-6575, on the Marginal. Ice cream, confectionery and snacks.
**Feira Popular** (People's Fair), Av. 25 de Setembro (entrance off Rua de António Fernande). Something to suit every palate.

### SHOPPING

Processed goods and luxuries available from *supermercados* such as **Complexo Shoprite** on the airport road. Guidebooks and maps are obtainable at the newsstand inside **Hotel Polana** and **Sensações** next to **Mundo's**, 657 Av. Julius Nyerere. **Tritute Batiks**, run by a women's co-op, is in a small side street off Julius Nyerere, close to Hotel

Avenida. **Artedif** (on Marginal) sells curios; buy traditional *capulanas* at **Casa Elefante**, opposite the Mercado Central.

### TOURS AND EXCURSIONS

**Rent-a-Car**: Mozambique Travel Service, Nelspruit, South Africa, tel: (+27 13) 751-2220, fax: 751-2220, info@mozam biquetravelservice.com www. mozambiquetravelservice.com/
**Dana Tours**: 729 Avenida Mao Tse Tung, tel: 49-7483, fax: 49-7428, info@danatours.net www.danatours.net/ For flights, car hire, hotels, tours.

### USEFUL CONTACTS

An excellent website is www.mozguide.com
**Teledata** is the main ISP: www. teledata.mz/ pages/agentes.htm
**Medical emergencies:** Clínica de Sommerschield, Av. Kim Il Sung, tel: 49-3924/5/6, fax: 49-3927. **Central Hospital**, tel: 42-0448, 42-0457, **Clínica 222 & Ambulance Service**, Av. 24 de Julho, tel: 222, **Dentist**, Dr Zaid Tayob, Av. Patrice Lumumba, tel: 30-8882.
**Specialist Travel Agency** (Johannesburg): Mozambique Connection, tel: (+ 27 11) 803-4185, bookings@mozcon. com www.mozcon.com
**Connection Time Internet**

Café, Centro Comercial Hotel Avenida, 657 Av. Julius Nyerere.
Mozambique **Telephone Directory** (*Lista Telefónica*) via Internet: www.tdm.mz/
**DHL Couriers**, 1622 Av. 25 de Setembro, tel: 30-7290.
**City Taxis**, Sr. António, mobile: 82 309 788, or 82 841 454.
**Police**, tel: 42-7343, 42-7575.
**Bureau de Informação Pública** (BIP), on the corner of Av. Eduardo Mondlane and Av. Francisco Orlando Magumbwe, tel: 49-0200, fax: 49-2622, bip@bip.gov.mz www.bip.gov.mz For bulletins, maps and books.
**Dinageca** (government surveyor), 537 Av. Josina Machel, tel: 32-1804, fax: 42-1460, www.dinageca.gov.mz Sells topographic maps (letter from Ministry required).
**Centro Cultural Franco-Moçambicano**, off Praça da Independência (Av. Samora Machel). Library, also dancing, music or films some evenings; tel: 31-4590, 31-4599 or 32-0787, info@ccfmoz.com Hours: Mon 14:00–18:00, Tue–Fri 09:00–18:00, Sat 09:00–12:00.
**Clube Naval**, Av. da Marginal, tel: 41-2690 or 49-7674. Yacht club, pool, restaurant.

| MAPUTO | J | F | M | A | M | J | J | A | S | O | N | D |
|---|---|---|---|---|---|---|---|---|---|---|---|---|
| AVERAGE TEMP. °F | 77 | 75 | 73 | 73 | 72 | 68 | 66 | 68 | 72 | 77 | 81 | 77 |
| AVERAGE TEMP. °C | 25 | 24 | 23 | 23 | 22 | 20 | 19 | 20 | 22 | 25 | 27 | 25 |
| RAINFALL in | 6 | 4 | 4.3 | 2 | 0.7 | 1.2 | 1.5 | 2 | 1.5 | 1.2 | 3 | 6 |
| RAINFALL mm | 150 | 100 | 110 | 50 | 20 | 30 | 40 | 50 | 40 | 30 | 75 | 150 |

# 3
# The Lagoon Coast

Like a string of jewels, Mozambique's **coastal lakes** stretch for 500km (311 miles) from **Ponta do Ouro** in the south as far north as **Inharrime**. Many lagoons and estuaries, like **Piti**, **Quissico** and **Poelela**, have been cut off from the sea by some of the world's tallest forested **sand dunes**. Others, such as the **estuaries** formed by the Tembe, Maputo and Umbelúzi rivers as well as stunning Lake (lagoa) Uembje at Bilene, are open to the sea, providing protected spawning grounds for the area's fish species.

Whether seeking solitude on the shores of a lake, casting for game fish at the 'Cape of Currents' close to **Závora Lodge**, paddling a canoe up the **Incomáti River** estuary, exploring the superb **coral reefs** from **Ponta do Ouro**, **Praia do Tofo** or **Morrungulo**, or taking a self-drive safari in the **Maputo Elephant Reserve**, this strip of tropical coastline promises surprises from the crest of every dune and around the next headland along each idyllic beach.

This is Da Gama's *Terra da Boa Gente* (Land of Good People) – a reputation still deserved today, nearly 500 years after the Portuguese explorer anchored off Inharrime and was showered with gifts by the locals.

The proximity to **Maputo International Airport** (from where light aircraft may be chartered) and the wide range of accommodation on offer make the Lagoon Coast an ideal starting point for a Mozambican adventure. Base yourself at one of the charming and ideally located resorts and lodges described in this chapter and from there explore the variety and haunting beauty of the lakes and lagoons and their flora and fauna.

## DON'T MISS

**\*\*\* Over 300 bird species:** from soaring eagles to wandering albatrosses.
**\*\*\* Diving:** virgin coral reefs stretch for 500km (311 miles).
**\*\*\* Swimming with wild dolphins:** off Ponta do Ouro.
**\*\* 'World's best' shark diving:** off Ponta do Ouro.
**\*\* Big game fishing:** off Inhaca Island and Ponta Závora.
**\*\* Canoeing:** along primeval Incomáti River estuary.
**\*\* Maputo Elephant Reserve:** elephants still frequent their ancient migratory trails.

**Opposite:** *The pool area of the Inhaca Hotel is the best place to be on a hot day.*

## INHACA ISLAND (ILHA DA INHACA)

Inhaca (pronounced Inyaaka) Island lies some 24km (15 miles) from Maputo at the entrance to the bay. It is named after the chief who provided refuge for the shipwrecked early Portuguese explorers. Inhaca was probably first sighted by Europeans in 1502, when **Vasco da Gama** undertook his epic voyage around the Cape of Good Hope in search of King Solomon's legendary mines. En route to India, Da Gama was rejoined by Luis Fernandes who had been separated from the fleet during a storm at the Cape. Fernandes told of his voyage up a great river (likely to have been the Incomáti) and a bay filled with whales. This is assumed to have been Delagoa Bay, which was later investigated by **Captain Lourenço Marques**.

Visitors arriving in their own boats are encouraged to visit the port captain, who will be able to direct them to curiosities like the market, Coconut Lodge and Lucas' Place.

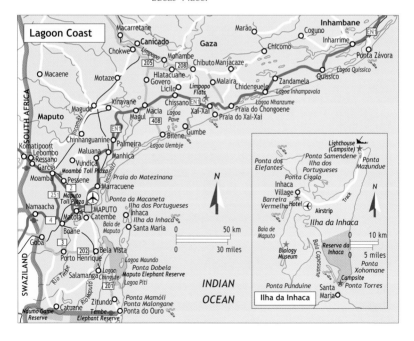

**Left:** *Fossils of giant marine snails such as this one have been found in Maputaland.*

## MAPUTALAND

Maputaland is (loosely) the geographical area that was controlled by Chief Maputa during the early 19th century and it extends from the southern shore of Maputo Bay down into South Africa as far south as the Lake St Lucia system. **Pontas Mamóli**, **Malongane** and **do Ouro** are tourist destinations all located in the Mozambican part of Maputaland.

The **Maputaland ecosystem**, with its plains, swamps, freshwater lakes and dune forests, is unique in southern Africa. Although the Maputo Elephant Reserve affords protection to a delicate habitat, the elephant migratory route from Tembe in South Africa, along the **Fúti Channel**, is threatened by slash-and-burn agriculture, as well as by commercial forestry. The Fundação Natureza em Perigo, in conjunction with the Peace Parks Foundation, is investigating the possibility of providing some official recognition and protection for this migratory corridor.

### Maputaland's Corals ★★★

Ranging in depth from 4m (13ft) to 12m (39ft), the brightly coloured soft corals (*Octocorallia*) and enormous stony corals (*Zoantharia*) in the waters off Maputaland provide a refuge for hundreds of species of brilliantly marked fish and crustacea. Emperor angelfish (*Pomocanthus imperator*) with their fingerprint stripes, freckled anglers (*Antennarius coccineus*) with their built-in lure, and painted surgeons (*Acanthurus leucosternon*)

---

**INHACA IS FOR THE BIRDS**

Inhaca's varied habitat attracts a great number of birds. On the island's western side, mudflats fringed by mangroves are frequented by a variety of water birds. A little offshore you will see hordes of gulls and terns including **lesser blackbacked gulls** as well as **Caspian** and **lesser-crested terns**. A jaunt on a fishing charter usually provides sightings of **white-chinned petrels** and **shy albatrosses**. Coastal bush on the eastern hills teems with the **gorgeous bush shrike, grey waxbill, trumpeter hornbill, green coucal, gymnogene, Neergaard's sunbird** and **yellowspotted nicator**. If it's introduced exotics you're after, **Indian house crows**, despite efforts to eradicate them, swarm around human habitation.

**Above:** *Snorkelling along Maputaland's reefs is a popular tourist pastime.*

with their bright blue body and yellow dorsal fin, as well as the huge but friendly, brown-blotched potato bass (*Epinephelus tukula*), are just a few of the attractions of Maputaland's reefs.

### Maputo Elephant Reserve ★★

Comprising 104,000ha (256,984 acres), the ***Reserva dos Elefantes do Maputo*** was proclaimed in 1960 in an attempt to protect the last of the herds which had been decimated by ivory traders over the centuries. The northernmost point of the reserve is the mouth of the Maputo River on Maputo Bay, while to the east is the open Indian Ocean. The peninsula that juts out towards Inhaca Island's Ponte Torres forms **Cabo de Santa Maria**, which is actually outside the park.

Mangrove and reed swamps dominate the northern reaches of the Maputo Reserve, while dense dune scrub and forests, interspersed with lakes Chingute, Maundo and Piti, cover the rest. The **Fúti Channel**, along which elephants migrate between Maputo and South Africa's Tembe Reserve, forms the western boundary. Maputo Reserve's 100 or so elephants are the last southern African herd still able to follow their ancient migratory routes, though poaching, slash-and-burn subsistence farming and commercial forestry are real threats.

---

**DIVING WITH GIANT TURTLES AND EAGLE RAYS**

The **leatherback turtle**, last survivor of the family *Dermochelyidae*, has a 200-million-year-old fossil history. Leatherbacks are the world's largest marine turtles, reaching 3m (10ft) in length and weighing in at an incredible 900kg (1990 lb). It is possible to swim alongside these living submarines by arranging a dive at one of the lodges on Mozambique's Maputaland coast.
**Ponta dos Elefantes**, off Inhaca Island, rivals the world's best dive sites, because here **giant eagle rays** (also called manta rays) often glide past the divers.

## PONTA DO OURO

The 'point of gold' (actually marked on some maps as 'Monte d'Ouro') which guided sailors for centuries, marks an unspoilt Mozambican beach that is easily accessible from South Africa and busy during the school holidays. High on densely forested dunes, the lighthouse overlooks the small curved bay where vehicles are only permitted to launch boats on a small section of the sand. The motel, chalets and camp sites are tucked under shady trees, and a constant sea breeze helps to keep the malaria-carrying mosquitoes at bay. Walk south around the point, a short distance down the beach to a tatty beacon, and stand with one foot in South Africa and the other in Mozambique.

### Diving at Ponta do Ouro ★★★

Within Ponta do Ouro Bay are five main dive sites from which to choose. Though corals are limited by the shallow depth (12–18m; 40–60ft) and the ocean surges, they do support a fantastic selection of fish life. Moray eels peer menacingly from holes, cowries display their colourful mantles, and the bright red tentacles of sea anemones ripple in the current.

### Ponta Malongane ★★

Another of the Mozambique coast's natural geographical beacons for enthusiastic divers, Ponta Malongane now marks the position of rich coral reefs. Here a small unprotected bay nurtures a coral wonderland.

> **THE PEOPLE OF MAPUTALAND**
>
> Often referred to as the **Tembe-Tonga**, Maputaland's inhabitants are actually made up of diverse clans and groups. Many fled to the area during the 19th-century reign of Zulu King Shaka, who skirted Maputaland during his raids. The Tembe-Tonga still prefer to speak Zulu; however, their customs are more closely related to those of the Tonga. Each homestead is built a discreet (but crucial) distance from the next, apparently to avoid quarrels with neighbours and the sometimes resulting accusations of witchcraft. Any visitor, even the chief or headman, must follow established rules of approach – standing well back until invited forward. Entrance into a hut requires permission from the owner.

**Left:** *A cloudburst threatens at the Ponta do Ouro border post into South Africa.*

**Right:** *Alfresco restaurant
at Ponta Malongane in
southern Mozambique.*

### Kev's Ledge ★★

On the northern part of the splendid Malongane reef,
at a depth of 24m (79ft), plates of hard **coral** hide
nocturnal **soldiers** (*Cheimerius nufar*), and **clownfish**
flirt with the poisonous tentacles of the **anemones**
which provide them with protection. **Saddleback
wrasse** (*Bodianus bilunulatus*) may be seen foraging for
sea urchins and crabs, which they crush using grinding
plates located at the back of their mouth.

### Ponta Mamóli ★★★

A short distance up the coast from Ponta Malongane,
Ponta Mamóli is a quieter, more intimate holiday spot.
Overlooking one of the finest beaches in southern Africa,
Ponta Mamóli Lodge (no camping) is tucked behind
casuarina trees and offers a fine restaurant and large pool.
Horse trails along beaches or into the trackless interior are
on offer. This is the last stop before the Maputo Elephant
Reserve and you will have to be fully self-sufficient if
you intend to camp at Ponta Milibangalala. There are a
couple of small stores at Ponta do Ouro village that sell
basic provisions, but it is wise to carry a good supply of
food, as places to the north of Mamóli are very isolated.

### Macaneta ★

The Macaneta Peninsula, on the northern bank of the
Incomáti River, is only 15km (9½ miles) from Maputo as
the crow flies. Unless you have your own boat to sail

into the mouth of the Incomáti River, the direction of approach is via **Marracuene**, 28km (17 miles) from Maputo. Cross the Incomáti River by ferry (which operates from 06:00–19:00). Travel 5km (3 miles) on a sand road and you will reach a trading store where you take the right fork to Macaneta Lodge, left to Jay's and Motapa Estuary Lodge. Two-wheel-drive vehicles will get through to the point with difficulty but no further.

### Jay's Lodge **

Secluded chalets, swimming pool and camp sites are hidden among the dune bush adjacent to Macaneta Beach. The fishing is excellent here and catches of kingfish and couta are common.

### Motapa Estuary Lodge ***

Rising near Bethal in South Africa's Mpumalanga province, and initially called the Komati River, the Incomáti crosses Swaziland before entering Mozambique at **Ressano Garcia**. On the inside of the wide meanders of the river's final bends, hidden among the dappled shade of marula and acacia trees, are tiny thatched fishing villages. Here Fernando Rodriguez, born in Mozambique but exiled by the past civil disturbances, returned to put a long-held dream into action, and constructed the Incomáti River Camp (now called Motapa Estuary Lodge). Determined to contribute to the rebuilding of Mozambique, Fernando used locally produced fittings and furniture wherever possible. Now under new manage-

> ### THE GENTLE SEA TURTLES
>
> Every year at the height of summer, **leatherback** and **loggerhead** turtles emerge from the sea at night as they have done for nearly half a million years. After dragging themselves above the high-water mark, they dig holes, lay a few hundred eggs, pack sand on top and disguise the nest by flinging loose sand around it. Although, in theory, Mozambique's beaches are protected, in reality a lack of resources renders the legislation meaningless and local people still hunt these magnificent, docile beasts. If you have the privilege of diving with one, please share this wonderful experience with other people, to increase an awareness of the turtles' plight throughout the world.

**Left:** *The idyllic Motapa Estuary Lodge, a place to relax and unwind.*

**Opposite:** *A quaint holiday villa, typical of those found at Bilene Lagoon.*
**Right:** *Camping under shady trees is possible on the Macaneta Peninsula.*

ment, the local people, who provide fresh fish, labour and handicrafts, have embraced the Motapa Estuary Lodge. The cosy bar and restaurant overlook a wide bend in the river and offer locally produced *cerveja dois em* (2M beer), *aguardente* (firewater) and delicious meals: feast on crab curry with cashew sauce, seafood with pasta and fresh tropical fruit salads, prepared almost entirely with ingredients available in the area. Accommodation at Motapa is in comfortable, mosquito-proof thatch-and-wood cabins, each furnished with two beds, bedside tables and easy chairs. Most have a raised veranda, from where guests can sit and contemplate the moods of the deep estuary as it rises and drops with the tides. The units are separated by indigenous gardens, which assure seclusion and privacy and are home to brightly plumed **sunbirds**. The lodge is decorated with paintings and crafts produced in Mozambique. Electricity is from a quietly humming generator, which is switched off in the evening. Light then falls silently from dozens of paraffin lamps.

The Incomáti River once emptied into **Maputo Bay** but was captured through erosion by the Massintonto River, and now curves northwards for 100km (62 miles), before turning back to Marracuene. Sediment at its mouth has formed a long sand spit which has broken up to form the **Xefina islands**. The reed beds along the banks, and the islands that dot the lower Incomáti, are refuge for hippos, crocodiles, dozens of species of water birds and massive mangrove crabs. Tidal for the last 30km (20 miles) of its

course, the river is an important spawning ground for fish and prawns, a situation that is exploited by subsistence fishermen. To walk through the reed-and-thatch villages perched on the high banks of the river is to experience a way of life that has remained unchanged for centuries. The combination of the beautiful Incomáti River and the long, empty Macaneta beach (the closest decent beach to Maputo) makes Macaneta well worth a few days' visit.

## BILENE LAGOON (LAGOA UEMBJE)

Due to its proximity to Maputo, Bilene is the main destination for *Maputenses* on holiday or simply taking a weekend break from the city. The town is neat, clean and offers a range of accommodation, restaurants and nightlife to the visitor. If loud Angolan music, hundreds of festive people downing beer on the beach and power-boats pulling water-skiers is your idea of a holiday, spend a weekend at Bilene. Weekdays, however, are usually very quiet, a chance for you to have the place to yourself.

To get to this pretty resort village with its 20km (12½-mile) long and 5km (3-mile) wide lagoon, take the EN1 for 160km (100 miles) north to **Macia**. Here turn right onto a good paved road, and continue for 30km (20 miles) to a traffic circle just after which you'll see **Hotel Bilene**. Although open for business, hotel staff may have trouble finding you a habitable room. Carry on downhill past the front of the hotel, turn left at the junction and carry on down to the 'marginal' or river road.

### IS BILENE LAGOON OPEN TO THE SEA?

Bilene Lagoon or, more accurately, **Lagoa Uembje**, is a favourite spot for deep-sea fishermen. The **Mozambique Current**, pushing powerfully through the Mozambique Channel, is at its closest to the coast here. **Longshore drift** carries sand from the north and deposits it in the lagoon mouth, often causing blockage, which is opened periodically by villagers who gather each summer en masse with spades. By the end of the rainy season (November–April), Bilene Lagoon usually fills to a point where it flows over the sandbar into the sea, thus flushing out the mouth. Ski-boaters, confined before to the sterile inland lake, can only then roar out to the fishing grounds in the open sea.

**Above:** *A carpenter in Xai-Xai produces another lovely piece of furniture.*
**Opposite:** *Time for quiet reflection at Lagoa Piti.*

## XAI-XAI

Perched on the northern bank of the **Limpopo River**, 224km (135 miles) north of Maputo, is the medium-sized town of Xai-Xai, the capital of Gaza province. Although severely damaged by the 2000 floods, Xai-Xai, with a population of over 100,000, has wide avenues lined with flamboyant trees, and offers ice (*gelo*), service stations, supermarkets, open-air markets, restaurants, international telephones, banks and a hospital. Clean toilets (a luxury anywhere in Mozambique) can be found at the first BP service station on your left, after crossing the toll bridge (when going south, a small fee is levied) over the Limpopo River.

### Praia do Xai-Xai ★

On the northern outskirts of Xai-Xai town, turn down to **Xai-Xai beach**, 10km (6 miles) away. A favourite fishing spot of South African anglers, Xai-Xai tends to be busy during the South African school holidays (June–July and December–January). The beaches here are long and clean, but due to its exposed position Xai-Xai has developed a reputation for being somewhat windswept.

Walking 7km (4½ miles) north from the developed area, you will encounter **Praia do Chongoene** with the abandoned Hotel Chongoene (now part of an ambitious new project). On the nearby beach are the remnants of a rusty shipwreck almost completely covered by sand. A large tidal pool known as **Wenela** (after a house owned by the recruitment agency of the same name), which overlooks the pool, lies 5km (3 miles) south of Xai-Xai beach. A large blowhole in the reef is exposed at low tide, but do beware of swimming near it due to the treacherous currents. To members of the African Pentecostal Church, Wenela is 'Jordan', a holy place where colourful baptism ceremonies are held.

### XAI-XAI'S JORDAN

The **African Pentecostal Church**, an organic blend of Catholic symbolism, evangelical zeal and African spiritualism, holds colourful and bizarre ceremonies at sacred spots. Walk south along the beach from Xai-Xai and you will come to a tidal pool fed by a tunnel. Here the brightly robed priests adorned with Catholic vestments and amulets made from herbs and animal parts hold noisy, complicated baptism ceremonies. One such ritual involves immersing women in the pool after which they are covered with chicken blood. This apparently is all in the name of 'cleansing' a widow in order that she be ready for marriage once more.

## THE LAKES

Most motorists just bypass **Quissico**, a 'one-street town' with a colourful market; but by bothering to go just 800m (½ mile) off the main road to Quissico's administration building at the end of a tree-lined avenue, you will reach one of the best viewsites in Mozambique. Azure-blue **Lake Quissico** (200m; 660ft) below, with its palm-fringed white beaches, stretches to the horizon from left to right. The darker shade of blue straight out in front, across high forested dunes, is the Indian Ocean.

### Lagoa Inhampavala and Praia do Chidenguele ★

Not visible from Chidenguele village, just off the EN1, this isolated stretch of inland water is surrounded by thickly wooded dunes. The beach (Praia do Chidenguele) lies only a short drive across. Herons, cormorants, flamingos and kingfishers inhabit the reed-fringed shores. Although the lake's water is pleasant for swimming, its high salt content makes it unpalatable for drinking. Sweet water can be collected from a spring close to where the road crosses the southern end of the lake.

### Ponta Závora ★

During South African and Zimbabwean school holidays, Závora is packed with sport fishermen and their families, so the facilities available fit the needs of this group. The reefs off Závora are reputed to offer some of Mozambique's best spearfishing opportunities. Camping is possible in a large area on the landward side of the dunes, with chalets on the seaward end. As there is a fair amount of swampland, mosquitoes can be a pest when the air is still. A small, well-stocked general store is always open. Fishing and diving charters may be organized by special arrangement, and an airstrip has been cleared.

> ### MOZAMBIQUE'S LAKE DISTRICT
>
> Stretching from **Chidenguele** on the EN1, 260km (161 miles) north of Maputo to **Ponta São Sebastião** further up the coast, a dozen freshwater lakes grace the coastline. From Inhazume and Inhampavala to Muangani and Manhali, these lakes show that Mozambique's coastline has periodically receded and advanced during a recent geological period. Tectonic forces as well as coastal erosion have combined to remove sand from some places, depositing it elsewhere, forming dunes, spits and sand islands.

# The Lagoon Coast at a Glance

**May–October** is the **coolest** and **driest** period. Average temperatures may remain above 20ºC (68ºF) but **cold snaps** do occur. **December** and **January** are **warmest**, but **high rainfall** (250mm per month) has a cooling effect.

From South Africa, if going further north than Bilene, you are unlikely to make it before dark due to border delays. Make your first stop in or near Maputo – the **Holiday Inn** on the Marginal (beachfront) or **Casa Lisa** north of Maputo (camping and chalets). Access to **Ponta do Ouro** and **Ponta Malongane**, though suitable for 4WD vehicles only (resorts collect visitors from the South African border), is from South Africa via Kosi Bay. Ponta do Ouro control post (safe parking for those being transferred by 4WD) is reached from Kwa Ngwanase (Manguzi) village. Then 11km (7 miles) through **deep dune sand** to Ponta do Ouro. From Maputo to the south, ferry (06:00–21:00) your car over to Catembe from the jetty, then cross the Maputo River to enter the **Maputo Elephant Reserve**, or go straight on to Ponta do Ouro. **Inhaca Island** is reached by speedboat and by air (*see* p. 43).

**Transportes Oliveiras** (*see* p. 42). Buses to Beira leave from the terminus (Praça 16 de Junho, Maputo) every morning at 05:00. For **Ponta do Ouro**, ask in **Catembe** for **supply trucks** going south. As these are unscheduled, be prepared to wait. **Air charter** companies: Moçambique Expresso (MEX), run daily trips to and from Inhaca Island and to other locations; tel: Maputo (21) 46-6008, fax: 46-5562, mobile 82 304 4770, mex@mex.co.mz www.mex.co.za Transairways, tel: (21) 46-5168, fax: (21) 46-5011, transairways@virconn.com The **EN1** (Estrada Nacional), in varying condition up to Caia (long sections are under construction until end 2006), is the main route north of Maputo.

### Inhaca Island
*MID-RANGE*
**Pestana Inhaca Lodge Hotel**, www.pestana.com/hotels/en/hotels/africa/InhacaHotels/Inhaca/Home/ Bungalow-style rooms, pool, restaurant.

### Ponta do Ouro
*MID-RANGE*
**O Lar do Ouro**, tel South Africa: 083 325 7026, Moz: (+258 21) 65 0038, info@pontadoouro.com www.africaninvitation.com/8060 Clichéd it may be but this is a real 'home from home' complete with swimming pool and restaurant.

*BUDGET*
**Tandje Beach Camp** (some-times called Ponta do Ouro Campsite), tel South Africa: (+27 11) 678-0972, rose@simply scuba.co.za www.simplyscuba.co.za A no-frills sprawling and fairly well-shaded camp site.

### Ponta Malongane
*MID-RANGE*
**Ponta Malongane Resort** (*Parque do Malongane*), tel: South Africa (013) 741-1975. reservations@malongane.co.za www.malongane.co.za Fully serviced chalets and rondawels – camp sites, restaurant, scuba diving and deep-sea fishing.

### Ponta Mamóli
*MID-RANGE/LUXURY*
Ponta Mamóli, tel: South Africa (+27 11) 444-3260, bookings@pontamamoli.com www.pontamamoli.com Horse out rides, scuba diving, whale watching, dolphin encounters, canoeing and deep-sea fishing. Fits in with the sensuous sweep of secluded beach (one of southern Africa's most picturesque). **Maputo Elephant Reserve**, 4WD, Mt200,000 entrance per person and per vehicle, Mt200,000 per person per day camping. **Ponta Milibangalala**. The only legal camping site in the Elephant Reserve. No booking.

### Macaneta
*MID-RANGE*
**Jays Beach Lodge**, tel Jacqui (Mozambique) mobile: (+258) 82 300 143, fax: (+258) 82 330 143. Access track through the

dunes is 4x4 only. A nice pool and an excellent restaurant.

### Marracuene
*LUXURY/MID-RANGE*
**Motapa Estuary Lodge**, tel/fax: (+27 15) 793-2200, www.imagineafrica.co.za/accommodationmotapa Intimate lodge on the Rio Incomati catering to a maximum of 8 people in comfortable en-suite chalets.

### Bobole
*MID-RANGE/BUDGET*
**Casa Lisa B&B**, 48km north of Maputo, tel: Moz mobile: (+258) 82 304 199, Buckland @teledata.mz Clean, secure family *casas* and camp sites.

### Bilene
*BUDGET*
**Complexo Palmeiras**, tel: (+258) 82 304 372 (Bella) or (+258) 82 895 4990 (João), palmeira@bilene.virconn.com http://palmeiras.no.ip.org Sandy camping sites, en-suite chalets and rondawels. Good Portuguese restaurant/bar.

*MID-RANGE/BUDGET*
**Praia do Sol**, on the lakeside 2km south of Bilene, tel South Africa mobile: +27 (0) 82 570 4300, leo@pdsol.co.za www.pdsol.co.za Secluded full-board chalets, full watersport centre, restaurant and bar.

### Zongoene (Limpopo River mouth)
*LUXURY*
**Zongoene Lodge**, tel Pretoria, South Africa: (+27 12) 346-

8868. Moz mobile: (+ 58) 82 391 194, info@zongoene.com www.zongoene.com Overlooks the mouth of the Limpopo. Luxury family and poolside Chalets. Separate 'Dunes Camp' and 'Casarão'. Camping (4x4 only).

### Xai-Xai (Praia)
*BUDGET*
**Parque de Campismo de Xai-Xai** (also called Xai-Xai camping site), tel: Mozambique + 258 (0) 22 35022 or Mobile + 258 (0) 82 7126520 (Nuno). Just metres from the beach and the breakers.

### Chidenguele
*MID-RANGE*
**Paraíso do Chidenguele**, tel Johannesburg: (+ 27 11) 782-1026, Moz mobile: + 258 (0) 82 729 5870, info@chidbeachresort.com www.chidbeachresort.com Thatched dune-forest chalets (self-catering) with timber decks and sea views, sleep 4–8.

Budget travellers can buy food from the *mercados* and *bazars* and fish from the beach (*praia*). Many resorts offer restaurants and/or self-catering.

### Ponta do Ouro
**Scandals**, next to 'Tandje' entrance. Open till 17:00, serves excellent sandwiches, pastries, pies, bread, cakes and salads.
**Café del Mar**, extensive menu, breezy and a memorable view.

### Inhaca Island
**Restaurant Lucas**, in Inhaca village. Traditional fare.

### Macaneta
**Restaurante Macaneta**, Macaneta Point, tel: (21) 65-0006. Pub; good seafood.

### Bilene
**Restaurante Estrela do Mar**, tel: (22) 59002, on beach road.
**Pavilhão Tamar**, Bilene, tel: (22) 59016. Open from 07:00, disco and Karaoke.

**Mozambique Connection**, tel: +27 11 803 4185, +27 11 803 6910, fax: +27 11 803 3861, bookings@mozcon.com www.mozcon.com Flights, lodges, etc. – 15 years of experience.
For luxury tours and camping safaris to the **Maputo Elephant Reserve**, contact the Catembe Gallery Hotel, reception@catembe.net www.catembe.net Swimming with dolphins on offer with **Dolphin Encountours**, www.dolphin-encountours.co.za

'Ask Mike' anything about Mozambique: www.mozguide.com For tailor-made packages, visit the website of **Mozambique Tours**, www.mozambiquetravel.co.za For scuba divers, a good contact is **Simply Scuba**, www.simplyscuba.co.za

# 4
# Inhambane
# and Surrounds

Inhambane province and its capital of the same name lie outside the destructive path of most of the tropical cyclones that can wreak havoc along the coast. The area's isolation has ensured its relative escape from modern influences; much cultural and historical heritage has been retained.

The **road** to the clean port town of **Inhambane**, a day's journey from Maputo, is tarred and largely in good condition, having been recently resurfaced and constantly maintained. Although at present no scheduled flights serve the town, the nearby **airport** is capable of handling **large jets** and is used by a number of South African and Mozambican air charter companies. Travellers with an **adventurous spirit** and no deadlines may want to try the (irregular) **dhow** traffic between Beira, Vilankulo and Inhambane. Although not the safest or most comfortable option, it is the most memorable. The jetties at **Maxixe** and Inhambane are the southernmost anchorage for Arab dhows, known as *ingalāoa* or *barcos as velas*, graceful ancient craft still being built in the villages lining the bay.

Within a 30km (18-mile) radius of Inhambane town lie at least a dozen destinations well worth a visit. From legendary **Linga Linga Peninsula** (no facilities) at the entrance to **Baia de Inhambane** (where **dugongs** are often spotted), Tofo beach (accessible in normal car) where Diversity Scuba offer a chance to explore the undersea world and the serene sands of **Ponta da Barra** to the prolific marine life of Paindane's beautiful **Lighthouse Reef**, and Guinjata Bay's comprehensive facilities, visitors can expect a cultural, culinary and historical feast.

## DON'T MISS

**\*\*\* Diving off Tofo and Ponta da Barra:** at Linga Linga diving with the gentle dugongs is unforgettable.
**\*\*\* Timeless Inhambane:** a friendly and fascinating town.
**\*\* Fishing:** marlin and sailfish can be caught from the beaches at **Pomene**.
**\*\* Snorkelling:** off Pandane lies a natural aquarium.
**\*\* Dhow taxi:** a unique mode of transport from Maxixe to Inhambane.
**\* Roadside stalls:** oranges and *lanhos* (young coconuts) for sale in summer.

**Opposite:** *Dhows lie at anchor in Inhambane Bay.*

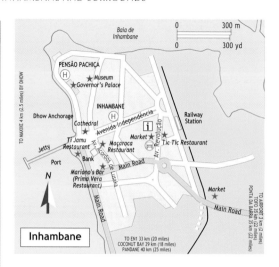

## INHAMBANE BAY

Travelling on the EN1, you will know you are approaching the provincial capital, Inhambane, when coconut palms begin to dominate the landscape. To reach the town, turn off at Lindela (unsignposted – watch for the 2M service station) and then continue for 33km (20 miles).

In the early 15th century, **Portuguese explorers** established a permanent trading post here, making Inhambane one of the oldest European settlements in southern Africa. Lying on the eastern shore of the large sheltered **Bay of Inhambane**, the sleepy and neat town has about 50,000 inhabitants. There is an **airport** suitable for large aircraft and the town also has **port facilities** capable of accommodating ships with a displacement of up to 10,000 tonnes.

Hundreds of graceful dhows on the usually tranquil water are one of Inhambane's most obvious features. The seamanship and boat-building skills of the *marinheiros* (sailors) and *pescadores* (fishermen) are legendary, and the town probably has the largest working fleet of dhows (around 200) on the East African coastline. Likely reasons for this statistic may be found in Inhambane's calm location outside (usually) the cyclone belt, as well as in the recent past when roads were often impassable.

Until the mid-1960s, Inhambane was a very crowded little harbour. The cranes on the jetty were kept busy loading tons of copra (coconut flesh), peanuts, oil seed, cotton, rice, sugar and cashew nuts. Those were the days when over a million migrant mine-workers commuted regularly between Mozambique and South Africa's gold-rich Witwatersrand (now Gauteng). A packet boat transported these men to the then Lourenço Marques from where they were taken to the mines by train. Although most of the area's produce is now transported to Maputo harbour by road, coasters still call at Inhambane on an irregular basis to offload consumer goods and load copra and cashews.

The Inhambane district is notorious for the brewing of powerful **illicit liquor** from cashews, pineapples, mangoes and oranges; in short, any fruit available. Known as *enhica*, the highly intoxicating effect of this concoction

### COCONUT REPUBLIC

The coconut palm (*Cocos nucifera*), of which there are nearly two million in the Inhambane area, produces about 22.5kg (50lb) of coconuts each year. Individual trees are owned by families, who send their youngest sons to collect palm sap for the production of a potent wine called *sura*. Inhambane's soil and climate are ideal for the palms – which only thrive in frost-free areas – so much so that trees take about five years to bear fruit (as opposed to seven in other areas), produce for about 40 years and live for up to 80. It appears that a rule of thumb is: 'the nearer the sea, the better the crop'.

**Left:** *Two Inhambane boys on a wide street look suspiciously into the camera.*

## A WORKING 'MUSEUM'

From Inhambane jetty walk down Av. Independência, right into Av. Acordos de Lusaka and a few blocks to the (now closed) **Prima Vera Restaurant** (Mariano's Bar) – next door is a fascinating working 'museum' – a printers called 'Gráfica sul do Save'. Politely ask permission to walk around this little **printing shop** that, far from being a formal museum, still produces such stationery items as invitations and invoice books. Every letter and character is first fixed on brass blocks and then placed by hand on manual presses. Most 60-year-old printing machines are regarded as antiques and displayed behind glass, but not in Mozambique. For decades all development stood still and so the country remains caught in a time warp.

on the locals is particularly noticeable during cashew season (from November to March).

When Mozambique was still a province of Portugal, **Antonio Enes**, a past governor general, referred to this moonshine as the 'root of vice and ruin'. One of his reports reads: 'In the season of this accursed fruit, when the atmosphere is poisoned by the resinous odours of the fat jugs displayed in the markets, and in the taverns, Native (sic) labourers leave their hoes, carriers abandon their loads, servants flee their masters, soldiers and sailors desert. Vagrancy and saturnalia continue so long as the supplies of drink last.'

A perfect *pensão*, a hotel, shops, markets, bus terminus and immigration office (in Maxixe across the bay) are all to be found in pleasant Inhambane. The dhows, fragrant spice and colourful cloth **markets**, **mosques** and little Indian-owned stores lend an exotic atmosphere to the streets. Inhambane Bay was the southernmost point down the Mozambique Channel to which **Arab** and **Persian traders** travelled. From about the 10th century until the mid-20th century, slaves, hardwoods, gold and other metals collected from the East African interior were exchanged for cloth, salt and beads.

**Left:** *The Cathedral of Our Lady of the Conception, in Inhambane, is 200 years old.*
**Opposite:** *A variety of goods is available from the market at Inhambane.*

### Sightseeing in Inhambane ★★★

Whether arriving by dhow, plane or car, visitors will inevitably end up at the *caias* or jetty, where the imposing 'new' **cathedral** (open Sundays – the 18th-century cathedral is behind it) and the long L-shaped **jetty** are obvious landmarks. Alongside the modern cathedral, the 200-year-old **Cathedral of Our Lady of the Conception** is worth entering. If you can trust the rusty rungs, climb up into the bell tower for sublime views of the bay and town. Avenida Independência stretches directly from the jetty; along this tree-lined thoroughfare you will come across the **Hotel Inhambane**, which, until renovated, should be avoided. **Garagem São Cristovão** sells petrol (*gasolina*), diesel (*gasóleo*), paraffin (*petróleo*) and engine oil (*óleo de lubrificar*). This service station is one of the few places around (Pachiça is another) where clean toilets and air to pump up your tyres are also available. You will pass major banks and the colonial-style municipal offices before reaching the large traffic circle at the end of the avenue.

Apart from Avenida Independência, three other avenues lead off from this circle. Straight ahead is the **railway station** and **shunting yard** where old locomotives stand and sadly rust away. Walk a little way up the quaint road called **Avenida Revolução** and you will find **Restaurante Tic Tic**, popular among the locals. The interesting municipal market, **Mercado Municipal**, close by is definitely worth an hour or two.

---

#### BASKET WEAVERS

Walk down Av. Revolução and a little past the **Restaurante Tic Tic**, and you'll reach the **Mercado Municipal**, a market that offers a bewildering selection of baskets, mats, hats and other useful household items. Prices are low by Western standards, but don't be tempted to pay more, as this only pushes prices out of reach of the populace. A **reed basket** is probably one of the most worthwhile purchases you can make as plastic bags are scarce, especially in northern Mozambique. Women cut reeds from the fringes of mangrove swamps and weave them while they are still green and pliable. Stroll into any of Inhambane's *bairros*, and you'll find the weavers sitting in front of their houses, hard at work.

Inhambane & Surrounds

Another picturesque street worth exploring, especially if you're hungry, is the **Avenida Acordos de Lusaka**. From the Inhambane jetty walk down the right-hand side of Av. Independência. One block down, turn right into the **Acordos de Lusaka** (don't expect to see any signpost) and drop into **Restaurante Maçaroca** a short distance down on your left. Another two blocks along this road, on your right, you will find the **Restaurante Prima Vera** (Mariano's Bar) where the 'city fathers' once regularly congregated. Mariano, the owner, weathered 50 years of change in Inhambane, but recently closed his bar.

If you walk from the jetty to the point you will pass the cathedrals, the governor's palace and get to Pensão Pachiça, probably the best accommodation in town and certainly the best place to get information about the area.

### Dhow Taxis ★★★

A short, cheap ride by **dhow** (the motor ferry, if faster, is usually dangerously overloaded), from Inhambane's jetty across the bay to the town of **Maxixe**, is a tempting alternative to the dusty, 62km (38-mile) trip around the bay by road. Backpackers disembarking in Maxixe from their buses will naturally opt for the wind-powered option, but if your party has arrived by car you may as well draw straws to see which one of you will have to do the driving.

You may have to wait till there are enough passengers to warrant the dhow's departure, so sample a few refresh-

**Above:** Dhow taxis line up for trade at Maxixe.
**Opposite:** A dhow offloads its passengers at the Maxixe ferry jetty.

ments at the **Snack-Bar Ti Jamu** (or at **Stop** if in Maxixe) at the beginning of the jetty – an ideal spot for admiring the dhows on the bay, especially at sunset. Adhering to a quaint tradition that dates back hundreds of years, the dhow crew will insist on carrying you to and from their boat, an old-fashioned service offered with such genuine enthusiasm that it would be impolite to decline.

Dhows are synonymous with Inhambane. Walk into any of the villages along the shores of Inhambane Bay that are accessible from the main road and you will come across skilled *carpinteiros* (carpenters) building new vessels using traditional tools and techniques that have been handed down for generations.

The origin of the name 'dhow' remains unclear, but what is known is that these craft originated in the seas off Arabia. The ocean-going variety, which displaced up to as much as 200 tonnes, was used for the slave trade until 1860. Today, dhows that big are very scarce, but the 'modern' ones still display the characteristic lateen (triangular) sail, a single, short wooden mast and a very long yard (crosswise spar) which is rigged at an angle of 45° when the vessel is under way.

## SHE-OAKS

The she-oaks or casuarinas (*Casuarinaceae*) are made up of a group of 45 highly distinctive semi-evergreen trees and shrubs native to northeast Australia, Southeast Asia, New Caledonia, Fiji and the Mascarene Islands. Casuarinas are tall trees with slender but wiry shoots which 'weep' (give off a light sap that soils tents, cars and anything else left underneath them). Common along the entire length of the coast, the Mozambican casuarina (*Casuarina equisetifolia*), also known as the horsetail tree, South Sea ironwood and she-oak, grows well in brackish soils, and was planted to stabilize the sand dunes and to form a windbreak. The name 'she-oak' derives from the resemblance of the tree's long thin needles to women's hair.

## DHOW RACE

Cowes Week is just a cruise around the dam compared to this spectacle of epic proportions. In **November** each year (some years are missed), the provincial governor sponsors a dhow race on **Inhambane Bay**. The competitors take this event very seriously as the prize money amounts to as much as a year's earnings. Plan to be in the area during the ***Corrida de Barcos as Velas*** and you could witness, or even take part in, this unique challenge (dhows are for hire).

## EXECUTION ROCK

Around the shoreline along Tofo beach is a grassy mound on a small peninsula. Short limestone cliffs drop into the ocean where waves shoulder the rock relentlessly. This is **Ponta Verde** and here stand the remnants of a sculpture glorifying the victories of Frelimo. Just beyond this structure is a deep, narrow gulley, where bones of the victims of 'kangaroo' courts (summary trials held without proper proceedings or witnesses) could be found. If you are willing to risk climbing down this crevice, you could still find the odd femur or skull. But if you slip, your skeleton might become a tourist attraction too!

## TOFO VILLAGE AND BARRA BEACH

Driving east from Inhambane, you will skirt mangroves and coconut plantations on the way to Tofo. When the wind blows through this seasonally busy fishing resort, it seems as though the voices of the ghosts of raucous big-game fishermen echo softly down the sandy streets. And yet Tofo has and still is changing, buildings have been renovated, the revamped and renamed (now once again called **Tofo**) hotel is open for business and the **Clube Ferroviáro** (Railway Club), Nordine's, Fatima's Nest and Bamboozi Lodges as well as Albatroz and Casa Barry, among others, now provide comfortable rooms and shady camp sites.

Visitors need not bring a supply of food as Tofo is well supplied with good eateries, some of which may be closed during the week in the low tourist seasons (Christmas and Easter are busiest). Tofo fronts onto a small bay fringed by a pristine, wide and white beach which stretches north as far as **Ponta da Barra** (Sandbar Point), and to the south, a short distance around a rocky headland, to a coral-lined bay called **Tofinho** where there is a nice surfing wave.

## BARRA PENINSULA AND CAPE INHAMBANE

When viewed from the air or on a large-scale map, Inhambane Bay in many respects resembles a river delta. However, the geomorphologic processes that have

produced the channels, sandbanks, island and spits that make up the Barra peninsula and Cape Inhambane have, in fact, worked in an opposite way to those producing deltas (where sand, carried to the sea by rivers, is deposited and the river subsequently splits into channels). At Inhambane Bay, the sand carried by the northward-moving long shore countercurrents is constantly being deposited at the mouth of Inhambane Bay. Sandbars form, in time becoming spits and small bare islands, ideal places for mangrove trees to colonize and thus stabilize. In this region the process is at an advanced stage, as seen by the extensive mangrove swamps between Inhambane town and Cape Inhambane.

As the seabed dips steeply away from the shore, causing large waves and therefore strong currents to enter the bay, Tofo can be a somewhat treacherous swimming beach for the unwary. Snorkellers and scuba divers who don't use the services of **Diversity Scuba** should always leave one of their party on the beach to summon help in an emergency, and limit their outings to periods when the tide is coming in. Bathers are warned to swim and surf only directly in front of the hotel as strong **rip currents** prevail on the left (when facing the sea). Surfing can be excellent if the tide is right at **Tofinho**, or 'little Tofo', around the headland to the right, before you reach the recently vandalized monument. It is also a wise precaution not to tempt the villagers by leaving any unattended belongings on the shore.

### Backpackers' Facilities ★★★
Independent travellers are well catered for by nearby **Fatima's Nest** and **Bamboozi Lodge** (4km north of Tofo)

**Opposite:** The hotel at Tofo is located right on the beautiful, unspoilt beach.
**Left:** Tofo Beach – paradise for sunbathers, swimmers and surfers.

**Right:** *Paindane Beach has some of the best snorkelling sites in Mozambique.*
**Opposite:** *The lovely stretch of coastline between Coconut Bay and Pandane.*

which has a great pub and food, but you'll be able to buy fish on the beach, and fruit and vegetables are sold at the *cruzamento* (crossroads) next to **Bar Babalaza** (local expression for the mother of all hangovers) 5km (3 miles) away towards Inhambane.

Note that the twin irritations of **mosquitoes** and petty thieving could ruin your stay, so remember to bring mosquito nets and repellent, and look after your kit. Always lock everything out of sight, in a vehicle if possible, and don't flaunt any valuable items.

### Horses at Ponta da Barra ★★★

The route to Ponta da Barra from Inhambane is similar to that to Tofo, but when you get to the *cruzamento* (look for Bar Babalaza), carry on straight onto a road which becomes increasingly sandy. Although accessible for skilful drivers in a kombi or pickup truck with the tyre pressure reduced to 100kpi (1 bar), Barra's many beach lodges are best accessed by 4WD.

Transfers from Bar Babalaza (guarded parking) are available by arrangement. No wheels? Then catch a *chapa* to the *cruzamento*, and hitch or walk the last 7km (4½ miles) to the beach. Wayne and Lillee of **Barra Lodge** and **Flamingo Bay**, who hire out the horses, and the folks of Barra reef will welcome you to their section of one of the most popular and beautiful beaches in Mozambique.

---

**MAURICE'S TALE**

Maurice, the **Ponta da Barra lighthouse keeper**, is full of tales of times gone by. He recalls the days when Portugal paid him and his lamps burned with paraffin; today the beam is solar-powered, and he is not sure who pays him. Like Maurice, many folk are not here simply for the fishing and diving, and if you are a visitor of the more curious persuasion, draw closer to the point: watch the sunrise over the water where two opposing currents meet; jog down to Tofo and back; walk along the beach to the mouth of the mangrove estuary and at low tide, walk into the swamp and marvel at this delicate, complex ecosystem.

## Guinjata Bay ★★

Guinjata is a great destination especially for the fishing, diving, boating and 4WD fraternity. Facilities are comprehensive and the almost exclusively South African clientele are well cared for – right down to a pub and toilets on the beach.

## Paindane (Praia de Jangamo) ★★

Paindane is an exciting and accessible **snorkelling paradise**. A superb inland reef (Lighthouse Reef), which is only a few metres deep at high tide, is protected from destruction by the powerful currents, waves and surges by a sand bar. Visibility under the surface is usually at least 20m (65ft) and in midsummer can be as much as 40m (130ft), making Paindane beach one of the very best snorkelling spots on the East African coast.

### MAXIXE AND SURROUNDS

About 460km (285 miles) from Maputo, Maxixe (pronounced 'Masheesh') is the only section of the EN1 that touches the long Mozambique coastline. Maxixe is therefore an obvious place for travellers to kick off

---

### SEA OF ZANJ

The Sea of Zanj or Bahr-el-Zanj lies between the Tropic of Capricorn and the Equator, from the east coast of Africa to beyond the Mascarene Islands (Mauritius, Réunion and Rodrigues). South African writer, T V Bulpin, wrote in 1957: 'In the Arabian Nights there was such a sea. Sinbad knew it well, although in after years its name was quite forgotten. It was a fabulous sea of countless islands, strange and magic. It was a sea which nursed a lost world inhabited by nightmare creatures wandering through a whole greenhouse of fantastic plants. It was a sea of legends where dwelt the Roc, that monstrous bird which, it was whispered, could carry an entire elephant in its talons. It was a mysterious wilderness of waters, a backblock of the Indian Ocean where the great rollers came sweeping in towards the shores of Mother Africa. It was the sea known to the Arabs by the ancient, long forgotten, but most honoured name of *Bahr-el-Zanj.*'

## DIVING WITH DUGONGS

Dugongs are increasingly rare but can still be found in East African coastal waters, and at **Linga Linga** divers may even be lucky enough to observe them underwater. The young are born off-white, but darken with age to a deep slate grey. The skin is thick, tough and smooth. They are sparsely covered in short hair, except for long bristles on the muzzle. Adults use their flippers for steering, and tadpole-shaped tails for propulsion. The mammals are aquatic herbivores, feeding on sea grasses, algae and crabs. Feeding typically occurs in water 1–5m (3–17ft) deep. Characteristic wear and tear on tusks and tails is attributed to rooting and digging. Breeding occurs throughout the year. The exact gestation period is unknown, but is thought to be about a year.

their travelling boots and get some of that sea breeze through their hair. Maxixe's jetty, just 50m (165ft) across the road from the Mobil service station, is one of the world's last major dhow staging posts. The EN1 passes between the town and the bay, so apart from the **Campismo da Maxixe** (camp site) all other facilities are on your left, if travelling north, and on your right, if travelling south. Alongside the EN1 there are brand-new service stations located on either end of the town's outskirts. You will be able to find limited spares and repair facilities in Maxixe.

## Ponta da Linga Linga ★★

Linga Linga is not to be missed if you have a (slightly) adventurous spirit and a desire to experience non-commercialized, uncomplicated Mozambique. Dhows leave for Linga Linga irregularly from the Inhambane and Maxixe jetties so get down to the waterline, put out word that you're headed for Linga Linga, and soon (could be the next day) a dhow will be at your disposal. For the same price per day as a dozen beers would cost you, a sturdy, seaworthy craft and crew will be at your disposal. If the wind is right, the trip

**Opposite:** *These rustic chalets at Campismo de Maxixe are inviting and comfortable.*
**Right:** *Passengers line up at the ferry jetty of Maxixe.*

will take three to four hours, but if it fails, prepare yourself for an uncomfortable wait. The sun is the worst enemy of becalmed sailors; so take along plenty of water and a *capulana* (sarong) to rig up for shade.

Linga Linga is the focus of some schemes to develop it into an ecotourist destination, but a lack of potable water and its remote location are hampering efforts. Be fully self-sufficient if you are heading here, and include enough drinking water (10 litres, or 20 pints, per person per day is recommended).

### Massinga ★

With its carpentry shops and colourful market, Massinga is worth a closer look on your way to somewhere else. The true significance of Massinga will only be revealed to those unfortunate enough to damage an essential part of their car in the area. Behind one of the two filling stations in Massinga, there is an excellent little workshop, where a **mechanic** (*mecânico*) does a fine job of welding together broken bits of suspension or chassis while you sip one of Rashid's wide variety of drinks at his restaurant, Dalilo.

---

#### CREATURES OF THE CORALS

Coral reefs provide a habitat for a large variety of organisms which rely on the coral for food and shelter. Decapod crustaceans such as **shrimps** and **crabs**, as well as fish like the **parrotfish** (*Scaridae*) depend on corals for shelter. **Sponges** inhabiting coral cavities as a protection from predators remove small chips of calcium carbonate from their hosts, thereby causing bio-erosion. Other organisms that inhabit the reefs are **crown-of-thorns starfish, sea urchins, jellyfish, clams, oysters, turtles** and colourful **sea anemones**.

**Right:** *Another hard day at Morrungulo Lodge!*
**Opposite:** *Waves roll into beautiful Nelson's Bay.*

### Morrungulo (Nelson's Bay) ★★★

This divine little **coconut grove** with its beach-fringed bay is primarily a sport fishing and diving location ideal for families. The first stunning views of the camping area are of lush green grass under gently swaying coconut palms – and a few steps away unspoilt, glistening white sands stretch in an arc from horizon to horizon. This is delightful Nelson's Bay, named after the Zimbabwean family who owned the resort before 1975, and who, by buying the coconut palms, managed to hold onto it through the dark years when the tourists stayed away. Old man Nelson died in 2004, but his son has taken over and is continually improving Morrungulo.

### Pomene ★★★

Pomene and Ponta da Barra Falsa are situated on the point of a large peninsula reached via a scenic track, negotiable for the last 5km (3 miles) by 4WD only. The once-famous hotel now lies abandoned and in ruins, but a wonderfully positioned lodge has now opened.

There are plans afoot to rehabilitate the Pomene complex and surrounds, but until then the facilities at Pomene Lodge, tucked between the mangroves and the deep blue sea, will do just fine. Pomene is special and Pomene Lodge is situated on a narrow sand spit which separates the lagoon from the sea, so that at the end of a day's fishing you can simply cruise right into the estuary and anchor against the jetty. Manager Errol recounted how, during one of the recent string of cyclones, he noticed that the main building of the lodge was preparing for take-off, so he grabbed the HF radio and headed for the old hotel on the point. When the hotel was abandoned in 1986, the housekeeper, one Judas Ammite, spirited away much of the precious crockery and cutlery and buried it in preparation for the return of his 'Padrão' (boss). Judas will show his stash on an island in the mangroves.

### SYLVIA SHOAL

In his book *Beneath Southern Seas*, Tim Condon writes of Sylvia Shoal (2km; 1⅓ miles from Morrungulo): 'They abound in everything the sea has to offer, and every moment is like a chapter out of a Jules Verne novel. Indeed, I sincerely believe that, until a diver has dived on Sylvia Shoal, he (sic) has never dived at all.' If the idea of diving with giant manta rays, docile whale sharks and big leatherback turtles appeals to you, then Sylvia Shoal, by all reports, is a good bet.

## Inhambane and Surrounds at a Glance

**April** to **September**, though still very warm, is the **cooler** and **drier** period. The area lies on the edge of the cyclone belt, so these rarely occur. **August** and **September** are often windy. **Hottest** and most **humid** (away from beaches) is **November** to **February** – when the risk of **malaria** is highest too.

Although Inhambane has an excellent airport, it is not served by LAM flights. **Air charter** is regularly arranged from Maputo (see p. 42), Nelspruit or Johannesburg. Transportes Oliveiras and Virginias **buses** travel to Inhambane regularly from as far south as Maputo and as far north as Chimoio and Beira. Since this town is 33km (20 miles) off the EN1 some buses stop only at Maxixe, from where dhows and motor-taxis (overloaded) cross every 30 minutes or so to Inhambane.

The tar road to **Tofo** is in good condition but access to most other beaches (Barra, Morrungulo and Závora excluded) is by 4WD or high-clearance vehicle only. **Route to Tofo and Barra**: Through Inhambane, 19km (12 miles) to the *cruxamento*); straight to Barra, right to Tofo. To get to **Coconut** and **Guinjata Bays** and **Paindane**, 21km (13 miles) after Lindela (the junction with

the EN1), turn right onto a sand track (4WD) – Coconut Bay is about 22km (13 miles) away, Guinjata 35km (20 miles) and Paindane Beach lies 3km (2 miles) further south. The turn-off to **Nelson's Bay** (Morrungulo) is 6km (4 miles) north of Massinga; 13km (8 miles) from the EN1 along a passable track you will come to Morrungulo's reception building.

### Inhambane
*BUDGET*
**Pensão Pachiça**, tel Mozambique mobile: + 258 82 355 9590 (Dennis), farolturismo @teledata.mz www. barralighthouse.com Large, double-storey house on the bay road (Marginal) near the jetty and dhow anchorage. Competent management, good food, ideal for backpackers, overlanders and families – dorm, doubles and bunks.

### Ponta da Barra
*BUDGET*
**Barra Reef**, tel/fax: Johannesburg (11) 867-3982, execupol @mweb.co.za Self-catering villas, camping and excellent ablution facilities.

*MID-RANGE*
**Barra Lodge**, tel Johannesburg, South Africa: + 27 (0) 11 314 3355, reservations@barra lodge.co.za www.barralodge. co.za All the ambience and facilities of a traditional hotel with pool and beach bar (and

restaurant). On-site scuba operator, horse riding.

*LUXURY*
**Flamingo Bay**, tel Johannesburg: (+ 27 11) 314 3355, fax: 314 3239, reservations@ flamingobay.co.za www. flamingobay.co.za Built on stilts (Maldives style) in the Mangrove estuary. Pool deck, restaurant, lounge and pub, luxurious chalets. It burnt down just after opening in January 2005 and is being rebuilt.

### Tofo
*BUDGET*
**Fatima's Nest**, tel: +258 (0) 21 302994, mobile: +258 (0) 82 307087, fatima@virconn. com www.mozambique backpackers.com Owned by the same Fatima of 'Fatima's Maputo Backpackers' fame. Indeed perched like an albatross nest on top of the dunes and so usually the wind keeps the mosquitoes away.
**Bamboozi Backpackers**, tel and fax Inhambane: +258 (0) 293 29040, mobile: +258 (0) 82 459056, bookings@ bamboozi.com www.bam boozi.com Relaxed, informal atmosphere, dorms and camping overlooking the beach.

*MID-RANGE*
**Casa Barry**, tel South Africa mobile: + 27 82 808 5523, fax: + 27 31 762 3469. Fully equipped dive centre: www. tofoscuba.com Spacious chalets, camp sites, huge bar/ restaurant – good family spot.

## Inhambane and Surrounds at a Glance

**Annastasea**, tel: +27 (11) 803
4185, fax: +27 (11) 803 3861,
bookings@mozcon.com
www.mozcon.com A Swahili-
styled very spacious and cool
compound for 12 people, and
4 en-suite rooms. A 20-minute
walk to the beach.

**Maxixe**
*BUDGET/MID-RANGE*
**Campismo de Maxixe**, tel/fax:
(293) 30351. Rustic beach
houses and 2-bed cottages,
camping and 'Overland Truck'
sites (with 220 V power). Boat
launching from the site.

**Inhambane Peninsula**
*BUDGET/MID-RANGE*
**Paindane**, Nelspruit tel/fax:
(13) 719-9772: Furnished
thatched *casitas*, camp sites,
an idyllic beach and an
inshore reef – excellent
snorkelling.
**Guinjata Bay**, proadven@
mweb.co.za tel: South Africa
mobile: 083 2836918, fax:
(13) 741-3149. Favoured fishing and diving destination for
South African families.

**Massinga**
*BUDGET/MID-RANGE*
**Morrungulo Resort**, no phone,
MG10@bushmail.net
www.morrungulo.co.za
Beautiful setting, secure camp
sites; well-equipped, self-
catering, 4-bed chalets.

**Pomene**
**Pomene Lodge**, bookings@
pomene.co.za www.pomene.
co.za tel: South Africa mobile:

082 7118161. Self-catering
chalets, well-spaced camp
sites. On a spit between a
pristine lagoon and a wild
beach – truly marvellous.

### WHERE TO EAT

Some resort restaurants may
only be open during peak
periods (Easter, Christmas, and
South African school holidays).
If self-catering, the municipal
markets (*mercados*) of Maxixe,
Inhambane and Massinga offer
a mouth-watering variety of
fresh fish, fruit and vegetables,
but be sure to bring processed
foods with you.

**Inhambane**
**Maçaroca**, 32 Rua Acordos
de Lusaka, tel: (293) 20489.
Close to the main avenue and
jetty – great Brazilian food.
**Pensão Pachiça** (*see* Where to
Stay). Dennis is the chef and
his pizzas are really good.
**Ti'Jamu** (Jamu's). Bay-side
(next to jetty) quaint
restaurant/bar/nightclub with
a great ambience.

**Tofo**
**Hotel Tofo**. Dine on delicious
lobster while sitting on the
cool front veranda watching
the waves.
**Albatroz**, tel: (293) 29005,
all-you-can-eat Sunday buffet,
also has chalets and camping.
**Dino's Beach Bar**, on the
beach, pleasant, but may close
during quiet periods.
**Restaurante Ferroviário**, more
options for vegetarians than
most places – tasty sandwiches.

**Maxixe**
**Stop**, tel: (293) 30025.
Esplanada, with superb view
of the bay and dhows.

**Massinga**
**Restaurante Dalilo**, where
Rashid offers a dozen brands
of imported beer, as well as
good soups and a memorable
piri-piri chicken.

### SHOPPING

The Inhambane market has an
excellent selection of colourful
traditional crafts. The Maxixe
market is one of the country's
busiest – fascinating, too.

### TOURS AND EXCURSIONS

For diving in the Inhambane/
Tofo area, **Diversity Scuba** is
based at Casa Amarelho,
Tofo Beach, tel: (293) 29002,
info@diversityscuba.com
www.diversityscuba.com
**Barra Lodge** (*see* Where to
Stay) arranges scuba diving,
sea-kayaking, horse riding
and excursions to places of
historical and natural interest.

### USEFUL CONTACTS

For general information on
the history and sites of
Inhambane city and sur-
rounds, contact **Melissa**
(thethirdparty@teledata.mz)
who organizes cultural
events, or go to the
**Nightclube Zoom** in
Inhambane and ask.
A reliable contact in the
Tofo/Inhambane area is
**Diversity Scuba**: www.
diversityscuba.com

# 5
# Bazaruto
# Archipelago

Africa's version of the famed Galápagos Islands, the Bazaruto Archipelago and surrounding marine environment is a complex and unique ecosystem, well protected by its isolation. Harbouring one of the last viable populations of dugong along the entire East African coast, the Bazarutos command some of the most pristine coral reefs in the Indian Ocean. In descending order of size, **Bazaruto**, **Benguerra**, **Magaruque**, **Santa Carolina** (also known as **Paradise Island**) and tiny undeveloped **Bangué Island** each have their own charm and character.

Amid the turquoise shallows surrounding each island, in the tidal inlets and shaded sea pastures opening into the deep Mozambique Channel, a wealth of marine life exists. For conservationists the uniqueness of this archipelago lies in its fragile diversity. Wildlife ranges from migrant bird species, **frigate birds** and **falcons** to **crocodiles** lurking in the brackish inland lakes. At least five species of **turtle** have their breeding ground here, while various **antelope**, rodents, lizards and snakes inhabit the massive mobile sand dunes and adjacent scrubland.

For the moment, only part of Bazaruto, Benguerra and a narrow strip of adjacent sea have been designated as a national park but it is hoped that co-operation between the WWF International, Endangered Wildlife Trust, Southern African Nature Foundation, International Wilderness Leadership Foundation and Lodge and Hotel owners will lead to a sound conservation management policy, uniting all the islands under the protection of a greater 'Parque Nacional do Arquipélago do Bazaruto'.

## Don't Miss

**\*\*\* Bazaruto Archipelago:** excellent scuba diving and snorkelling on Two-Mile Reef.
**\*\*\* Funazi Dhow:** go to 'Sail-Away' near Vilankulo's hotel Dona Anna.
**\*\*\* Charter cruises:** fabulous trips around the islands.
**\*\*\* Vilankulo village life:** witness a traditional wedding or wander around the *bazars*.
**\*\* Big game fishing:** record-breaking catches of sailfish.
**\* Baobab forests:** the southernmost occurrence of these in Mozambique.

**Opposite:** *A fisherman carefully inspects his net at Benguerra Island.*

## CLIMATE

As the islands nestle inside the curve of the mainland, the archipelago and adjacent coastline experience a similar **tropical** climate. The area has a lower rainfall than places further south of the Tropic of Capricorn, such as Inhambane and Xai-Xai. Vilankulo experiences maximum daily temperatures of 32°C (90°F) in December and January, while rainfall is around 150mm (5in) during each of these months. **Humidity**, while at uncomfortable levels during summer (**September–May**) on the mainland, is always bearable on the exposed islands and beaches. **Evenings** during **July** can be **cool** enough to prompt the donning of a light sweater.

**Opposite:** *A boy from Vilankulo proudly shows off his unusual catch.*
**Below:** *This village near Vilankulo is close to the lovely beach.*

## MAINLAND TOWNS
### Vilankulo ★★

About halfway between Maputo and Beira, Vilankulo has become an important public transport and air terminus. It lies only 21km (13 miles) off the EN1 and 10km (6 miles) from **Magaruque Island**, which makes Magaruque that much more accessible from the mainland. An international airport (visas can be issued here on arrival) with a tarmac runway of 1300m (4300ft) serves the town. Taking this as well as the newly surfaced road into account, Vilankulo is fast becoming the mainland's gateway to the **Bazaruto Archipelago**. Developers are taking advantage of its location by opening lodges, backpackers' facilities, restaurants, camp sites, hotels and boat charters. In addition, Vilankulo is well supplied by a dhow safari operator (**Sail-Away**), market, bank, public phones and Internet, service stations, quaint supermarkets and a medical clinic. Lounge in a lodge, set up your tent, install yourself in one of the rustic huts, stock up on *mandioca* and lush papaya (pawpaw) fruit and forget about shopping malls!

In order to orientate yourself it is advisable to get down to the Art-Deco **Hotel Dona Anna** (due for renovations), which overlooks the harbour. Once reopened, the hotel's shady *esplanada* (veranda) will offer a cool refuge from the midday heat. From Hotel Dona Anna, turn right (south) along the beach road (don't walk alone in this area at night). A 20-minute walk takes you to a shady and clean camp site which also offers basic chalets. Have a cold drink and check out the *casas* (huts) at breezy **Quiosque Tropical**, and then carry on to **Casa da Josef e Tina**. Backpackers and other independent travellers should carry on for another five minutes or so to characterful **Zombie Cucumber Backpackers**, one block away from the beach.

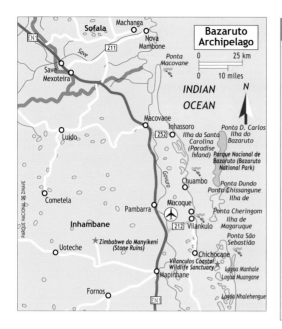

Map: **Bazaruto Archipelago**

Sofala, Machanga, Nova Mambone, EN1, 211, Save, Ponta Macovane, Mexoteira, 0 25 km, 0 10 miles, INDIAN OCEAN, N, Macovane, Inhassoro, Luido, 252, Ilha da Santa Carolina (Paradise Island), Ponta D. Carlos, Ilha do Bazaruto, Parque Nacional de Bazaruto (Bazaruto National Park), Govuro, Chuambo, Ponta Dundo, Ponta Chissangune, Ilha de, Cometela, PARQUE NACIONAL DE ZINAVE, Pambarra, Mucoque, Ponta Cheringom, Ilha de Magaruque, Inhambane, 212, Vilankulo, Zimbabwe do Manyikeni (Stone Ruins), Ponta São Sebastião, Uoteche, Chichocane, Vilanculos Coastal Wildlife Sanctuary, Mapinhane, Lagoa Manhale, Lagoa Muangane, Fornos, EN1, Lagoa Nhalehengue

In need of assistance and information? A short distance south from Zombie Cucumber you will find *Paraiso Serviços* owned by long-time resident of Vilankulo, Margie Toens, tel: + 258 (0) 293 82228.

Still haven't found what you are looking for? Start again at the Dona Anna, and this time drive (or walk) to the left, north around the palm-lined bay, where dhows and other small boats anchor and old ships are left to die. A sandy road leads past a few crumbling buildings, swings a little away from the beach, and heads out of town, still following the edge of the bay. Persist on this indistinct route and you will reach Casa Rex, which has great rooms and excellent food. At the end of this 4km-long sandy road you will find **Aguia Negra** (Black Eagle) and **Vilanculos Beach Lodge**, both offering some of the most comfortable accommodation in Mozambique.

The managers of lodges and campgrounds can assist with accommodation, information, fishing and diving as well as water sports, island boat cruises and provisions.

**Above:** *Magaruque Island Lodge offers accommodation in an idyllic setting.*

### Inhassoro ★★

Inhassoro is a sleepy little **fishing village** some 94km (58 miles) to the north of Vilankulo and just 15km (9 miles) from the EN1. It has a service station, but the pumps often run dry. Inhassoro boasts a camp site with seasonal scuba and fishing facilities, two hotels (*see* p. 86), a bus terminus, a few restaurants, general stores, a marketplace, a health post offering basic nursing service, a police station and a short grass airstrip a stone's throw from the *bairros*, so expect goats and children to be hazards if attempting to land here.

### THE ISLANDS
### Sail-Away (Funazi Dhow) ★★★

Just down from the Dona Anna and one road up from the beach, Dave and crew and their dhow called *Funazi* offer fully catered authentic dhow camping safaris, which include the islands of the archipelago. Sail with men who have grown up on the sea. An unpretentious, genuine experience capturing the essence of Mozambique.

### Ilha de Magaruque ★★

Circumnavigating Magaruque on foot is a leisurely three-hour stroll along deserted white beaches. The ambience of the island is relaxed and intimate. Once revamped, Magaruque Island Resort will offer full board and lodging, and a choice of rooms, bungalows and chalets.

Magaruque has the advantages of a paved airstrip, superb **snorkelling** or **scuba diving** on a coral reef just a short swim from the front of the hotel, and ease of access from the mainland. Transfers in **ski-boats** to and from Vilankulo are available by prior arrangement, and there are always **dhow rides** for the adventurous.

---

**ORGANIZAÇÕES JOAQUIM ALVES**

Prior to the independence of Mozambique in 1975, **Senhor Joaquim Alves** of Vilankulo ran a small fleet of coasters, a chain of trading stores in the Vilankulo area, an air transport company and owned the **Hotel Dona Anna**, named after his wife. Senhor Alves also held the tourist concession for the entire Bazaruto Archipelago, and operated **Hotel Inhassoro** and the bungalows at the resort at **Bartolomeu Dias**, some 48km (28 miles) north of Inhassoro. The islands are now a national park, the hotels in need of repair, Bartolomeu Dias has slipped beneath the waves, and Senhor Alves would be about 100 years old, if alive today.

### Ilha de Benguerra ★★★

Since Benguerra is blessed with the most intact area of **indigenous dune forest** of all the islands, it probably offers the best **birding** as well. Crocodiles, which must already have been resident when the island separated from the mainland several thousand years ago, also populate freshwater lakes, surrounded by stunning golden dunes. Apart from the shelters of a great many migratory fisher folk who use Benguerra as a seasonal stopover, there are the comfortable **Benguerra Island** and **Marlin Lodges**, as well as a convenient 800m-long (875yd) grass airstrip.

### Ilha da Santa Carolina (Paradise Island) ★★★

*Pérola do Indico* ('Pearl of the Indian Ocean') the Portuguese called it, but it will always be just **Paradise Island** to those who have enjoyed its isolation.

About 3km (2 miles) long and roughly 500m (547yd) wide, from the air the tiny island resembles an athletics track. The 100-room **hotel** was derelict for decades, but the ever-optimistic staff sometimes offer visiting yachts people a meal on the veranda, and talk of a time when their *padrão*, or former Portuguese boss, would finally return. The most recent developments on Paradise involved the partial restoration of the hotel annex, but visitors should expect nothing and be fully supplied down to drinking water. Visitors can arrange to arrive by boat from Vilankulo or Inhassoro.

**SAND DUNES SURROUNDED BY SEA**

The three larger islands (Bazaruto, Benguerra and Magaruque) were once joined, forming a 70km (42-mile) sand spit moulded by a combination of wind action, changing sea levels and longshore current drift. This giant sand dune broke into four bits some 6000 years ago (Santa Carolina, a rocky outcrop, had separated from the mainland 120,000 years previously). Only Santa Carolina is a true rock island surrounded by deeper water – a better anchorage than Benguerra and Bazaruto. Magaruque has a deep channel near the lodge but, with a tidal range of 4m (13ft), low tide leaves most of its beaches a long way from the sea.

**Above:** *A flock of flamingos sweeps gracefully over Benguerra Island.*
**Left:** *Tourists on the* Kingfisher *fish the blue waters around Benguerra.*

### Ilha do Bazaruto ★★★

About 30km (18 miles) long and some 3km (2 miles) at its widest, Bazaruto is the biggest island in the archipelago. Parallel with the mainland, on its northern point where the *Farol do Bazaruto* (lighthouse) still flashes its signal out to sea, there is top-class tourist accommodation in the form of the **Bazaruto Lodge** and **Indigo Bay Hotel**.

The island is served by a grass airstrip near the Lodge and a new tarmac strip next to Indigo Bay capable of handling twin-engined aircraft. In the event of the strips being dangerous to use (which sometimes happens during the rare thunderstorms), you would land in Vilankulo and be transferred to your destination by boat. You will have to beach some distance from the lodge if you don't happen to arrive at high tide, but will be taken to the lodge by Land Rover.

### Island Fishing ★★★

Bazaruto Island, as well as Benguerra and Magaruque, are attracting increasing numbers of saltwater fly fishermen (and women); the sight of someone standing etched against a golden sunrise, gracefully casting their line out over the waves, is a vision as ancient as the sand itself.

Crossbars on which catches of the day could be hung up, weighed and photographed once formed a focal point of the island experience but are rarely used nowadays. Today's environmentally friendly fishers prefer to weigh, photograph and tag their trophies before releasing them alive and kicking back into the blue. Conservation and rehabilitation of the environment is uppermost in the minds of lodge owners and management, who are campaigning to have the archipelago declared a World Heritage Site.

Of added interest to nature lovers are the southern lakes, which are inhabited by **freshwater crocodiles** and a few elusive species of endemic butterfly.

**Below:** *Many fishermen visit Bazaruto Island in the hope of landing the Big One.*

**Left:** *Although many land mines have been cleared throughout Mozambique, they remain a potential hazard and motorists are advised not to veer onto unknown tracks.*

## EN ROUTE TO BEIRA

Most motorists from South Africa don't travel further north than Vilankulo. This was once due to the poor condition of the EN1 between Vilankulo and Beira, as well as a lack of service stations and accommodation. Times have changed; the EN1 is being regularly maintained as far north as the Beira corridor, and has now been extended as far as Caia on the Zambezi. There are **fuel stations** at **Vilankulo**, at the turn-off to **Inhassoro**, at **Muxúnguè** (128km/80 miles north of Save) as well as at various places on the Beira–Zimbabwe road. Mapinhane marks the turn-off to Zinave National Park and the Pafúri border post (South Africa) and it has fuel, basic accommodation and food at **Restaurante Boa Viagem**.

Apart from the EN1 that is tarmac, and the road to Nova Mambone, **minor roads** to and along the coastal area between Inhassoro and Beira have not yet been upgraded, and may be impassable during the November to March rains. There are many river crossings, and ferries may not be operational, while forgotten **land mines** will be a hazard for some time to come. Hire a local guide, who knows the tricky areas, to show you around.

Even though **Sofala** is one of the country's oldest settlements, visitors anticipating being able to scramble among romantic ancient ruins will be disappointed. Shifting sand dunes have obliterated the site of the former fort, but the unspoilt beach is charming enough to attract self-sufficient sun-seekers and fishermen.

### SOFALA, ANCIENT OPHIR OF THE BIBLE?

Known to Arab sailors since biblical times, reference to **Sofala** is made in Milton's epic *Paradise Lost*. Desperate to boost their lagging economy, the Portuguese crown embarked upon a frenzied search for what it believed to be the legendary golden city of **Ophir**. In 1501 the Portuguese established a permanent presence at Sofala. Apart from a few gold beads, though, the treasure trove did not materialize and the surviving settlers returned home empty-handed. In 1904 stone from Sofala's old fort was used to build a cathedral in **Beira** – an apparent act of vandalism until one realizes that the ancient site was being obliterated to such an extent that today there isn't a trace left of the fort's foundations.

## Nova Mambone *

Accessible via a brand new tarmac road from **Mexoteira** on the EN1, 18km (11 miles) south of the Save River, Mambone is the **prawn capital** of Mozambique. Silt carried down by the **Rio Save** as well as the mangrove swamps in the area provide an ideal breeding ground for the crustaceans. Mambone is not often visited by travellers, but **Jaime's Hotel** and some basic restaurants are ready to receive guests. If you do venture to these shores, bring along a small boat – the mouth of the Save is a fascinating place to explore and the beach is inaccessible by car.

## Save River Bridge *

To cross over the Save River Bridge you have to pay a small toll. Also, have your vehicle papers and driver's licence ready, as police may want to examine these here. Stop to stretch your legs and buy a few fresh bread rolls and cold drinks, and relax in the shade overlooking the beautiful river valley. The 258km (160-mile) stretch between **Save** and **Inchope** (on the EN6 between Beira and Mutare in Zimbabwe) is lonely, remote and beautiful. Apart from the Muxúnguè BP, and the odd logging camp where you might find water and diesel (at a price), don't expect any facilities.

When using this and other remote routes in Mozambique, common sense dictates that you travel in a convoy of two or more cars, carry extra fuel and water and a comprehensive set of vehicle tools and spares such as fan belts, radiator hoses, fuses and a puncture repair kit. Also, be sure to depart early in the morning, as night driving on potholed surfaces frequented by unlit trucks and tractors can be very dangerous.

## Espungabera to the Coast *

The only west–east route which is a feasible option in central Mozambique south of Beira is the wild, rugged and yet scenic track that begins at the **Mount Selinda–Espungabera frontier** post with Zimbabwe (it is open 09:00–16:00).

The first 105km (66 miles) to the ramshackle town of **Dombe** traverse the southernmost reaches of the beautiful sandstone **Chimanimani mountain range**, where you may come across leopard, eland and baboon. The **Lucite River crossing** at Dombe is facilitated by a small hand-winched pontoon which often becomes inoperable during the December to April rains, when the river is too strong to negotiate.

From Dombe the track winds alongside the lazy Lucite River for 60km (37 miles) until it intersects with the much wider EN1. If you have sufficient fuel to cover a further 400km (250 miles), sticking strictly to the well-used course for fear of land mines, cross the main road and continue on the final 120km (75 miles) parallel to the Búzi River, through Goonda and Nova Almada to the village of Búzi. This is an important agricultural centre which is served by motorized ferries from Beira on an irregular basis, but usually about twice a week. Some of your party could take the ferry to Beira, while the driver reaches the city via Inchope. The boat-trippers can be collected at the small **Mananga boat harbour** in the *baixa,* adjacent to the historic building of the Manica Beira Company.

### MAGICAL MUSIC OF THE *MBIRA*

Andrew Tracey, Professor of African Music at South Africa's Rhodes University in Grahamstown, has visited the area between the Búzi and Save rivers in search of the enchanting tunes played by the **Ndau people** on their *mbiras*. The mbira is a small wooden instrument with metal keys. Played with the thumb and index finger, it produces a sound similar to that of a tiny tin harp. Some of Mozambique's most influential mbira virtuosos hail from the **Machanga** region (to the north of the Save's mouth) and the adjacent offshore islands of **Nyanguwo** and **Chiloane**.

**Left:** *Tired after a long day's hike, these backpackers are glad to reach the relative safety of this overnight shelter in the Chimanimani mountain range.*

## Bazaruto Archipelago at a Glance

The beaches here are usually cooled by **sea breezes** which moderate the high summer humidity (September–May). From November to March the average monthly **rainfall** is above 200mm (8in) and **high temperatures** (35°C; 95°F) and 100% **humidity** can make conditions uncomfortable; however, visibility for divers is usually best at this time.

At present there are scheduled LAM flights to Vilankulo from Maputo, while Pelican Air flies to and from Johannesburg on a daily basis. All of the islands have airstrips served regularly by **Pelican Air**. **Vilankulo** has a small airport (being extended) suitable for large turboprop aircraft. **Inhassoro**'s short bumpy strip is only used by bush pilots. By road, both Vilankulo and Inhassoro are only a few minutes away on tar from the EN1.

Transportes Oliveiras and Virginias **buses** service the area, and **dhows** (for adventurous folk with unlimited time) sail irregularly between Inhambane and Vilankulo and from Vilankulo to Inhassoro and the islands. **Speedboat** and **dhow** transfers are available between the archipelago and Inhassoro or Vilankulo. *Chapas* operate between the mainland towns. **Paraíso Serviços** in Vilankulo

do airport transfers and vehicle hire, margie@teledata.mz

### Vilankulo
*BUDGET*

**Zombie Cucumber Backpackers** is the best bet for backpackers and independent overlanders. No bookings possible. Mozambique tel: +258 82 8049410, steph@ zombiecucumber.com www.zombiecucumber.com
**Tine e Josef** (no phone), on the beach road 2km south of Hotel Dona Anna. Self-contained *casas* (small houses), good food prepared for guests.

*MID-RANGE*

**Casa Rex**, tel Moz: +258 23 82048, fax: +258 23 82425, casarex@teledata.mz Views of the dhow anchorage and the Bazaruto Islands. Jungley wild-island garden, steps straight down onto the beach, highly rated restaurant. Garden, family and courtyard rooms and a luxury (honeymoon) suite.
**Blue Waters Beach Resort**, tel: +258 293 84030, mobile: +258 82 8075750, bluewater @tdm.co.mz 6km south of Vilankulo – a quiet, lush setting on the beach. Lots of space between chalets, generous camping area, restaurant, bar.

*LUXURY*

**Vilanculos Beach Lodge**, tel: Cape Town, South Africa: +27 (0) 21 691 1763, fax: 691 1764, beachlodge@vilanculos. co.za www.vilanculos.co.za

Secluded chalets, good restaurant, service and facilities – scuba diving and water sports.

### Inhassoro
*BUDGET/MID-RANGE*

**Hotel Seta**, tel/fax: +258 (0) 293 91000/1/2, mobile: +258 (0) 82 849400. Seaside chalets, spacious *casas*, shady camping area, good ablution facilities. Dining/entertainment complex, mahogany trees shade a breezy patio. Secure, peaceful.
**B. D. Lodge**, Ponta Bartolomeu Dias, tel: + 258 84 390 5700, fax: +258 293 91012, bdlodge@mozadventures.com www.mozadventures.com 30km north of Inhassoro. Chalets have their own central kitchen, dining area and bar for self-catering. Restaurant specializes in seafood.

### Bazaruto Island
*LUXURY*

**Indigo Bay Island Resort**, tel: Johannesburg, South Africa +27 11 467 1277, fax: 465 9623, reservations@rani resorts.com www.indigobay resort.com Part of the Rani group: www.raniresorts.com Well suited to folk who want to be pampered, entertained and kept busy while on holiday.

*LUXURY/MID-RANGE*

**Bazaruto Lodge**, tel: Mozambique, Maputo: +258 21 305 000, fax: 305 305, reservas. africa@pestana.com www. pestana.com First to be built on the island – probably the nicest location on Bazaruto.

## Bazaruto Archipelago at a Glance

### BUDGET
**Zenguelema Campsite** (Park HQ), very basic – bring own food and drinking water.

### Benguerra Island
#### LUXURY
**Benguerra Lodge**, tel Johannesburg, South Africa: +27 11 452 0641, fax: 452 1496, benguerra@icon.co.za www.benguerra.co.za Fits in seamlessly under a forest canopy along a perfect beach. Big refurbishment includes honeymoon chalets and restaurant/bar/socializing area.
**Marlin Lodge**, tel Pretoria, South Africa: +27 12 543 2134, fax: 543 2135, reservations@marlinlodge.co. za www.marlinlodge.co.za Aimed at the serious big-game fisherman, full scuba service. Sea-facing chalets with private patio and walkway to beach.

#### MID-RANGE
**Gabriel's Lodge**, tel: +258 (0) 82 3894250. Locally owned and managed – basic two-bed chalets and restaurant. Bring in a few drinks and non-perishable foods.

### Magaruque Island
**Magaruque Island Lodge** is due to be renovated soon.

#### WHERE TO EAT
All of the island resorts and coastal lodges can offer a full-board service. Forget about the diet before you arrive – the food is healthy and scrumptious.

### Vilankulo (Vilanculos)
**Vilanculos Beach Lodge** (see Where to Stay), good seafood in a cool setting.
**Casa Rex**, excellent breakfasts; try their seafood platter lunches and dinners.
**Smugglers**, www.smugglers. co.za Where the 'expats' (in Vilankulo read South Africans and Zimbabweans) like to discuss rugby and politics. New poolside bar.
**Na Sombra** (shade), unusual woven-mat structure, good service and food.
**Quiosque Tropical**, on the beach – offers simple but tasty fare, cool on humid days.

### Inhassoro
**Hotel Seta** (see Where to Stay). Meals on offer at this restaurant range from fish with chips and fresh salad to prawns and coconut rice. Slow service.
**Complexo Salema Mufundisse Chibique**, friendly and good value for money.

#### SHOPPING
ATMs and banks operate in Vilanculo. Near the Hotel Dona Anna there is a shop displaying local crafts. As is the case in the rest of the country, the municipal markets are the cheapest (if you bargain) and most interesting places to shop. December to March is good for mangoes, papayas, pineapples, bananas and avocados, while June–September is the season for oranges, *naartjies* (tangerines), tomatoes and corn-on-the-cob. Coconuts all year round.

#### TOURS AND EXCURSIONS
Lodge guests will be able to occupy themselves with a variety of water sports including **sailboarding**, **snorkelling**, **water-skiing**, **game fishing** and **scuba diving**. A luxurious 56ft catamaran, the *Free Spirit*, based at Aguia Negra, offers cruise packages. Vilankulo-based Sail-Away (Funazi Dhow) run a very seaworthy dhow to the Bazaruto Islands (camping) – highly recommended. Ask for Dave and crew at their base in a house near the Hotel Dona Anna. Alternatively, speak to one of the **dhow** owners down on the beach to make the necessary arrangements. But beware of sudden gusty storms, especially during the cyclone or typhoon season from December to April.

#### USEFUL CONTACTS
**Paraíso Serviços** – there is no better person to ask anything and everything about Vilankulo than Margie Toens, tel: +258 (0) 293 82228, margie@teledata.mz Professional up-to-date advice is available via www.mozguide.com Vilankulo and Inhassoro have at last been linked to the outside world by telephone. In South Africa, the Mozambique specialists are **Mozambique Connection**, tel: +27 11 803-4185, fax: 803-3861, www.mozcon.com

# 6
# From Beira to Tete

Beira (capital of Sofala province) and Tete (capital of Tete) are the largest towns in Mozambique's central and western region, respectively. Both are historically and architecturally fascinating, owing their existence to the need for trading outlets: **Tete** is a Zambezi River port and **Beira** a busy ocean harbour at the mouth of the Púngoè and Búzi rivers. Tete's two squat sandstone stockades reveal its former 'frontier town' status, while dhows, handcrafted nearby, still ply Beira's ultramodern docks.

In this region the Mozambican Plain narrows, giving way to the Mozambican Plateau and the **Chimanimani**, **Gorongosa** and **Bvumba mountain ranges**. Mangrove swamps still occur sporadically along the coast, but corals are restricted by the shallows produced by a widening continental shelf, as well as the influence of silt deposited at the mouths of the Búzi, Púngoè and Zambezi rivers.

Extensive **mangrove swamps** occur between Beira and Nova Mambone, and around Quelimane. For birders this habitat is significant – it harbours rare species like the **palmnut vulture** and elusive **mangrove kingfisher**, found in greater numbers here than anywhere else on earth.

**Gorongosa National Park** has reached an advanced stage of restoration and can now accommodate casual visitors who are able to fend for themselves. Supported by a grant from the Carr Foundation (www.carrfoundation.org), plans to reintroduce the once-vast herds of elephant, buffalo and other wildlife and to extend the park's original boundaries are progressing. The raw romance of Africa retains a tenuous grip in this region.

## DON'T MISS

**★★★ Rio Savane:** a secluded wilderness beach resort 40km (25 miles) north of Beira.
**★★★ Praça do Município:** enjoy an espresso here.
**★★ Johnny's Place:** the oldest restaurant in town.
**★★ Mercado Municipal:** shop here for tropical fruit.
**★★ Macúti Beach:** fascinating shipwreck and lighthouse.
**★★ Bique's:** restaurant and (rustic) camping on Macúti Beach.
**★ Lambada:** dance at **Estrela Vermelha** or **Clube Oceana**.

**Opposite:** *En route to Cahora Bassa you will come across many traditional villages like this one.*

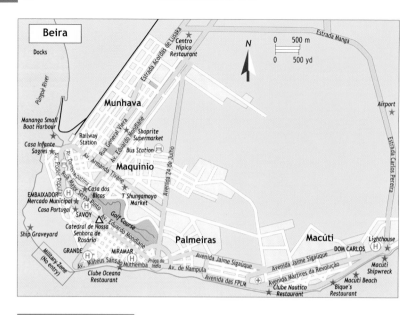

## CLIMATE

Central Mozambique is **hot** and **humid** in the coastal regions and hot and dry in the interior. Tete clings to the banks at the bottom of the Zambezi's heat-trapping valley. Average July temperatures in Tete rarely drop below 28°C (83°F), while **rainfall** ranges from 150mm (6in) in **January** and **February**, to a completely **dry May** to **June**. Beira's location on the coast, with cooling sea breezes and moisture-saturated air, gives it a slightly cooler but somewhat wetter climate than Tete. Beira is warmest from October to March, and experiences rain throughout the year, with December to March being the wettest months.

## BEIRA

A fairly large, important but neglected port city situated at the mouth of the Púngoè River about halfway up the country's coast, Beira is Mozambique's second city after Maputo.

Beira's origins lie in the historic settlement of **Sofala** which is a short dhow trip down the coast. Sofala was an Arab trading outpost for hundreds of years, where gold, ivory and slaves were exchanged for cloth and dyes, beads and spices. About 500 years later, Portuguese navigators, including Vasco da Gama, sailed into the estuary formed by the Rio Púngoè, to see if there was any truth in the story that gold was to be found in Sofala. It was not until 1881, when the European powers accelerated their colonial expansion into Africa, that the site was considered important enough for the Portuguese to establish a military garrison. Coincidentally, the Portuguese crown prince Dom Luis Filipe, who was born at roughly the same time, was given the title Prince of Beira. The new settlement was named in his honour.

Then the British, desperately seeking a sea outlet for landlocked southern Rhodesia, cast their eyes upon Beira. The British 'Chartered Company' troops clashed with Portuguese soldiers on a number of occasions in this area, while at the same time Portuguese traders began to explore Lake Malawi. Hostilities were finally ended with the signing of the **Anglo-Portuguese Treaty** of 1891, which, at last, defined the political boundaries of modern Mozambique and her neighbours.

During this period, the town of Beira was nothing but a stinking, fever-ridden mangrove estuary where malaria and dysentery ruled. Most of the early residents braved disease in search of their fortune during the frantic 'Manica gold rush'. Governor General Enes is recorded as saying this of the new arrivals: 'Ten or twelve pounds a month was paid in order to live, baked by slow heat between sheets of galvanized iron ... a visitor to the taverns of Beira, could hear veritable concerts of curses and blasphemies from the disillusioned, calling down fire from Heaven upon those who had deceived them with false hopes of wealth.'

### PRAÇA DO MUNICÍPIO

Since most buildings around the Praça do Município date from the colonial era, visitors may feel as though they were in the south of Portugal. During the day, the **municipal square** with its large central water feature, and **municipal offices**, which have a marble mural of the old Sofala fort in the hallway, are the social focal point for Beira's more affluent residents. Surrounded by **coffee shops** with tables under the trees on the pavement, the praça's ambience is more Iberian than African.

**Below:** *The busy harbour of Beira is port of call for a variety of vessels.*

## T'SHUNGAMOYO

*T'Shungamoyo* means 'courage' in the local **Ndau** dialect. Whether the informal markets in Beira reflect a brave attempt at prosperity or allude to their precarious legal status, the markets are referred to as T'Shungamoyo. The lively **Mercado do Goto** is a colourful sprawl of stalls selling *capulanas*, clothing, motor spares and electrical goods. Should the crowded chaos prove to daunting, a more tame market to explore is the **Mercado Municipal** in central Beira, the town's original colonial market.

The first impression on arriving in the *bairro Maquinino* on the city's outskirts may not be very favourable, but once you get over it, Beira holds hidden rewards for the inquisitive visitor. Beira is drab, dirty and chaotic, but it is also bewitching. Although the city is a lot smaller than Maputo, it was strategically far more important than the national capital during the civil war period (1977–92) due to its central location.

Beira's buildings display a mixture of colonial excess, bland postwar American and constrained socialist functionality in addition to the tin, cardboard and reed shelters of rampant unplanned urbanization.

The imposing **Railway Station** overlooks Praça dos Trabalhadores, where the parking space available far outstrips demand, as passenger trains no longer do the 300km (180-mile) journey between Beira and Zimbabwe. The oddly grandiose station has a cavernous entrance hall, high arched ceiling and ornamental fishpond. Overlooking this echoing, empty space is a clean and cool restaurant with an interesting menu and wine list.

A walk along the beachfront reveals what will become an enormous challenge to future city engineers: the sea is gradually undermining Beira's foundation.

**Below:** *The ferry at Caia is a vital mode of transport across the Zambezi River.*

## Beira's Architecture ★★★

The beautiful **Catedral de Nossa Senhora de Rosário** (Cathedral of Our Lady of the Rosary) on Avenida Eduardo Mondlane was commissioned in 1907 and completed in 1915. Stone from the old Portuguese fort at Sofala was used in its construction. Services are held every day.

The **Clube des Chinês** building, erected in 1917, was designed in the neoclassical style. Extensive renovations are now complete and it is once more one of Beira's finest structures. Originally a club for Chinese settlers, it now houses the city archives.

The quaint **Casa Portugal** (Portugal House) with its tin roof is a private residence located off Praça do Metical next to the **Banco Standard Totta**, and is typical of the turn-of-the-century colonial period.

**Above:** *The old-world charm of the Casa Portugal in Beira is captivating.*

Its high stone walls topped with battlements, the old **Prisão da Beira** (Beira prison) resembles a medieval castle. It lies just off the Praça do Metical and appears still to house criminals. Family members of the prisoners used to bring food to the inmates on a daily basis.

Don't miss the avant-garde exhibition hall named **Casa dos Bicos** after the sharp points on its roof (*bico* means beak or point) located on Av. Eduardo Mondlane.

Near the old golf course, on the way to the Praça da India, the Cinema São Jorge seats 1200 people and is one of the largest and most ornate cinemas in Africa.

Be sure to look at the **Casa Infante Sagres** on the west end of Avenida Poder Popular. This neoclassical building now houses Dalmann Furniture, Acisofala consultants and the Manica Mozambique Company, which was responsible for its renovation.

## Mananga Small Boat Harbour ★★

Wooden fishing vessels and ancient, rusting trawlers rub shoulders with each other here. More than just a safe place to anchor, this floating village houses a special community of honest fishermen but becomes a mud flat at low tide.

---

### THE LATE, GREAT HOTEL GRANDE

When it was erected near the mouth of the Púngoè in 1952, the **Hotel Grande** was Beira's most impressive structure. Today, sadly, it is a derelict high-rise squatter camp where goats meet you at the entrance and trees grow from balconies. Urban legend has it that, at independence, the hotel was handed over to the people by the socialist government, but this is not the case. From the outset, the hotel's tariffs were too high and too few wealthy tourists visited Beira to make it pay. The Grande has not received any guests since 1963, 12 years before Frelimo assumed power.

## Art Galleries ★★

There are quite a few interesting art galleries around. Visit the **Centro Cultural Português Pólo da Beira**, 148 Rua António Enes, <u>icamoes. ccbeira@teledata.mz</u>; the **Coroas de Moçambique**, which has a fascinating range of traditional musical instruments as well as some fine hardwood sculptures; there's also the **Co-operative Artesanato 25 de Marco**, specializing in commissioned works of art; the **Sociedade de Escultures 25 de Setembro**, where sculptors sit and chip away at wood and ivory outside their shacks; and the **Casa da Cultura**, 1314 Rua Major Serpa Pinto, a theatre-restaurant that hosts theatre groups and exhibitions.

## Mercado Municipal ★★★

The municipal market, just a few paces away from the Praça do Município, is one of Mozambique's most colourful and best-stocked marketplaces. Fruit and vegetables arrive by the truckload from as far afield as Maputo, Quelimane, Zimbabwe and Malawi, while dhows and chugging trawlers bring in fish, prawns, calamari (squid) and other food from the sea. Tiny stalls sell anything from toothbrushes to tinned tuna, and many splendid local crafts such as figurines in *pau-preto* (ebony) and *pau-rosa* (mahogany) are also on offer. Have you ever dreamed of mangoes the size of footballs, bananas as big as your forearm and pineapples too heavy to pick up with one hand? At Beira's Mercado Municipal those fantasies may become a reality!

## Macúti Beach, Shipwreck and Lighthouse ★★

The *bairro* of Macúti, one of Beira's wealthier residential areas, is named after a trawler that was wrecked nearby during a cyclone in 1917. It could seem ironic that the skeleton of the *Macúti* should have ended right beneath the lighthouse that was supposed to guide it to safety, but the hull was, in fact, towed there to act as a breakwater. Macúti beach extends some distance to the north and south of the lighthouse, and it is here that Beira's residents come to swim and promenade on weekends. Walk up past the lighthouse to where gaily painted wooden fishing boats lie hull up and the fishermen lay out their nets for repair. This is the best place to buy Beira's famous **prawns**, as well as a mouth-watering variety of other fresh seafood. The lighthouse is in good condition, and still accommodates the keeper and his family.

Take a look at the **Dom Carlos Hotel** behind the lighthouse, which was Beira's five-star flagship before independence but is now deserted except for a few loyal staff. Although the building is crumbling, the hotel's personnel have been waiting patiently for 30 years for the return of their boss. They will welcome you, if you don't mind the lack of running water and electricity and don't believe in the ghosts that are said to haunt the premises.

A word of warning: only venture out in groups after dark, as muggings have become a problem in this area.

**Opposite:** *Beira's Praça do Município is just a few paces away from the market.*

**Below:** *The* Macúti *was towed in front of the lighthouse to form a breakwater.*

**Right:** *These Shona women are crossing a bridge over the Púngoè River on their way home.*
**Below:** *A gifted Makonde sculptor carves away at his next work of art.*

### The Ship Graveyard ★★

From Praça do Município, walk west in the direction of the Púngoè River, past an informal market which specializes in selling clothes. On your left there will be warehouses and beyond them a large open area which must be avoided as it is a **military zone** (*zona militar*). Walk into the informal scattering of thatch-and-reed huts and watch out for the rusty steel prow of a ship sticking up from the shore of the river. Vessels that were sabotaged by the Rhodesian Special Air Service in 1977 or had sunk due to being unseaworthy have been towed here and abandoned.

Not only is this ship graveyard a monument to the follies of war and bankrupt socialist policies, it is also an amazing photo opportunity. Don't wave around your camera, though, as it could be stolen. Nearby you can see wooden ships being built according to ancient designs.

### Makonde Sculptors ★

Sculptors from the fiercely independent Makonde tribe of Cabo Delgado province have set up a small co-operative where Av. Martíres de Revolução meets Av. das FPLM. Their small run-down shack has a storeroom and a showroom where statues, traditional weapons and musical instruments are displayed. Much of the artists' work has been toned down to suit the taste of tourists – the real Makonde art is characteristically bizarre and surreal.

**Left:** *These eerie-looking masks were fashioned by Makonde artists.*

## Lambada Dancing ★

One of the more colourful and frivolous legacies of the Portuguese period in Mozambique's history is that of Latin-American dancing (a favourite with the temperamental, fun-loving Portuguese) which is popular at some nightspots. From 21:00 onwards, one of the places to be in Beira is the **Clube Oceana** in Av. Mateus Sansão Muthemba, on the beachfront halfway between Praça da India and the derelict Grande Hotel.

For a slightly younger vibe, take your dancing shoes to the **Estrela Vermelha**, situated a short way along the highway to Dondo, Chimoio, Manica and Zimbabwe.

## Remarkable *Rio Savane* (Savane River)

Located about 40km (25 miles) to the north of Beira on the Savane River is one of Mozambique's most peaceful resorts – Rio Savane. This mangrove estuary is almost pristine and the new owners offer boat trips up the river, and have seen buffalo, elephant and lion on their beach. During rain it is recommended that only 4WD vehicles attempt the drive past an old leper colony to the guarded parking area from where a motor-dhow transfers guests to the cottages and camp sites. Coming from Dondo the EN8 road reaches a flyover and turn-off to the airport. A short distance before the airport sign, turn left down a small track which passes through villages and after a few junctions terminates at Savane.

---

### THE STRIPED WATER DOG

*Hydrocynus vittatus* translates as 'striped water dog' but is known to countless fishermen as the **tiger fish**. Its Latin name is apt – it roams fresh tropical waters, attacking lesser fish. The tiger is lord of central Africa's inland waterways, but it is this contempt for invaders that is its undoing. Man, with rod and artificial lures, casts the bait into the tiger's territory and the aggressive predator attacks without reserve. Once hooked, the fish erupts into a sprint near the water's surface, broken by leaps into the air as it attempts to rid itself of the irritation. Once a fisherman has had a fighting tiger on the end of his line it is not only the 'water dog' that is hooked!

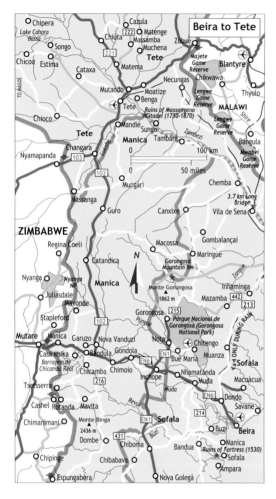

**Beira to Tete**

## En Route to Tete

In an effort to decrease Mozambique's dependence on South Africa's infrastructure, roads between Beira and Chimoio (192km; 119 miles), and Chimoio to Tete (389km; 241 miles) were resurfaced. This impetus (apartheid in South Africa; civil war in Mozambique) may have gone, but the road remains in good condition. (But beware of pedestrians, animals and potholes.)

As in most of central and northern Mozambique, fuel and repair facilities are scarce, but there are service stations in Beira, Dondo, Mafambisse, Nhamatanda, Chimoio, Tete andCatandica. Because of animals crossing the road, unlit vehicles and stationary trucks, driving at night is not recommended. To go to **Zambézia province**, you can drive to **Caia** on the old road via Inhaminga or now on the new road via Gorongosa town. Note that there is a 22-tonne ferry at Caia, and construction of the $80 million bridge over the Zambezi has begun. When driving in all built-up areas, assume that the speed limit is 50kph (22mph) and drive accordingly or risk a hefty spot fine. To go via Inhaminga, a short distance out of **Dondo** take the turn-off right onto the EN213; to take the Gorongosa option, turn right at Inchope, 128km (80 miles) from Beira.

**Opposite:** *Chitengo camp in the Gorongosa National Park is once again able to receive visitors.*

## Gorongosa National Park ★★★

The town of Gorongosa is near its namesake, Gorongosa National Park. Chitengo camp lies off the route on the newly extended EN1 (*Estrada Nacional* or national road), 78km (48 miles) from Inchope (turn right at Nota, 5km after crossing the Púngoè River). Visits to the park are possible once more: land mines have been lifted, fences re-erected and some game reintroduced. For information on where to spot wildlife, seek the local English-speaking crowd who congregate at **Bique's** (pronounced 'Beeky's') on Macúti Beach. The DNFFB wildlife authorities have set up basic facilities, including showers and toilets for visitors at renovated **Chitengo camp**. Note that you'll have to be self-sufficient during your stay and that the park is closed from 31 October to 1 May due to seasonal flooding.

## Chimoio (formerly Vila Pery) ★★

Once a resort for wealthy Beira residents, now a farming centre (many ex-Zimbabwean commercial farmers have settled in the region), Chimoio has mild winters and warm summers. Two service stations on the bypass off the EN6 offer fuel, repairs and a selection of spares. Chimoio also has supermarkets, banks, a post office, library, museum, central market and international telephone and Internet office (*telecommunicações*) at Complexo Shoprite on the EN6. Weary travellers can hang up their battered boots at the simple but comfortable **Pink Papaya Backpackers** or the more pricey **Hotel Executive Manica**.

### GORONGOSA'S WILDLIFE

Of the Big Five, only elephant and buffalo are commonly spotted by visitors. Rhino have disappeared and leopard do occur, but are exceptionally human-shy due to past poaching. Lions, were mercilessly hunted during the past strife, but are making a comeback and are sometimes found slinking around their old haunt, *Casa dos Leões*, the ruins of the original rest camp. Herds of rare sable and roan antelope, zebra, impala, kudu and eland, as well as the odd elusive cheetah, also roam across the park's vast expanse. The Gorongosa's bird life could well be labelled the 'little five hundred' as this is approximately the number of species occurring in the area.

### DR LIVINGSTONE, I PRESUME

The famous missionary and explorer Dr David Livingstone left the shores of West Africa in 1854 on a mission to claim territory for God and for Queen Victoria. After visiting the falls on the Zambezi River, which he named after his monarch, he vanished for months and was feared dead. In 1856 he emerged from the bush, haggard and ill, and was welcomed by the Portuguese at **Tete**, where he spent a few months convalescing. During this time he explored the area and noted the existence of surface coal diggings and alluvial gold panning.

## BALANCING ROCKS

Millions of years ago, immense pools of molten silica, magnesium, iron and other minerals and metals thrust close to the earth's surface by tectonic forces, began to cool. Surface forces of water, waves, wind and ice gradually scraped away the covering layers until the now solid granite batholiths and laccoliths became exposed in places. Expansion due to decreasing pressure had caused deep, uniform cracks which were widened by chemical and mechanical weathering processes. Along sections of the **Catandica–Changara** road these formations resemble immense building blocks piled high by a playful giant.

**Below:** *Villagers, like this woman in Chimoio, still live in traditional mud-and-straw huts.*

## CHICAMBA REAL DAM

Heading towards Zimbabwe on the EN6, skirt Chimoio and carry on past the **Changara** and Tete junction from where the turnoff to the dam wall is a further 13km (8 miles). A good gravel road turns left up a steep hill and passes through picturesque little **Chicamba village** where you can stock up on fruit, vegetables and dried fish. From a vantage point near the dam control room you have unimpeded **views** of the entire dam. See whether you can spot the lodge and crocodile farm at Casa Msika, on the opposite bank.

Approximately 50km (31 miles) from Chimoio, and 20km (13 miles) from Manica if coming from Zimbabwe, the turnoff to **Casa Msika** is marked by a clear sign on a stone wall. Stay at the fine lodge or camp site, have a chat with the fascinating owner, Peter Thornicroft, paddle on the lake or fish for bass, visit the crocodile farm and walk through the bird-rich miombo (*Brachystegia* sp.) woodland. The beaches of Lake Chicamba, dotted with the skeletons of dead trees, are eerily scenic.

**Barragem de Chicamba Real** (Chicamba Real dam) is built on the confluence of the Revué and Msika rivers. Until local residents returned from refugee camps in Zimbabwe and netted the lake's fish, sport fishermen from South Africa and Zimbabwe were catching record-breaking bass and carp. Nevertheless, a fishing competition may still be held annually during September.

From the top of the hill, follow the road down to the river. Cross it and you will see the 125m (410ft) concrete wall on your right. From here the road leads out of the small valley to the water's edge, where you may find an enterprising fellow operating a **restaurant** and *quiosque* from a converted ocean transport container. A short distance behind this unusual roadhouse lies a makeshift parking area. Here

**Left:** *En route to the Cahora Bassa dam, the traveller will encounter many traditional villages.*

you'll be able to launch a boat (with a little help from the locals), although a better **launching site** lies on the opposite side of the lake at Casa Msika.

From the turnoff from the EN6 to the EN102, which leads to Changara and Tete, it is 62km (38 miles) to a brand-new concrete bridge over the Rio Púngoè, 6km after which look for the Catandica Ranch signs (rooms and camping) and then a further 60km (37 miles) to the small town of **Catandica**, where you are able to refuel and purchase a few refreshments at the little store.

**Changara** lies 485km (301 miles) from Beira and 95km (59 miles) from Tete at the junction of **Estrada 102** and **Estrada 103**, which formed part of the infamous **Tete Corridor** of the war years. There is cell reception, but no operational service station or acceptable accommodation at Changara at present.

### SONGO AND LAKE CAHORA BASSA

About 128km (79½ miles) upstream from Tete, the beautiful Kebrabassa rapids once thundered unhindered through an almost inaccessible gorge. As early as 1957, when Mozambique was still a province of Portugal, a commission investigating the development potential of the Zambezi River valley recommended the construction of a dam for irrigation purposes and flood control. Kebrabassa was the site chosen, and plans for a formidable hydroelectric power station were finalized

---

**MSIKA HOUSE**

Hard times often serve to develop qualities of resilience, adaptability and ingenuity. Ex-Zimbabwean **Peter Thornicroft** found himself trying to survive in the midst of Mozambique's post-independence struggles, and excelled. Gaining a concession to farm on the shores of undeveloped **Chicamba Real**, Peter began to exploit the thousands of crocodiles that inhabit the lake. With meat at a premium due to devastated cattle herds, 'Senhor Crocodilos' as he was nicknamed by his staff, obtained a government contract to supply crocodile meat to the troops guarding the Beira Corridor. More recently he built a tourist lodge, **Casa Msika**, which caters for international visitors seeking to fish the ample stocks of bass and bream, as well as Beira businesspeople on a weekend's escape from the steamy humidity of the coast. Ironically, Peter died of malaria in 2004.

in 1960. On-site accommodation and amenities were urgently needed for the hundreds of workers, engineers and technicians who would build the gigantic dam and the turbines – thus Songo was born.

Today the village is still a busy settlement. Its entire population is employed by the HCB (**Hidroelétrica Cahora Bassa**) and visitors are only allowed entry if they present their passport at the control point.

**Songo** has a hotel, social club, filling station, post office, hospital, supermarket and paved airstrip with immigration. If you approach the HCB offices in Songo (can be arranged at Ugezi camp), you can go on a fascinating guided tour of the power-generating plant and dam wall.

### Fishing on Cahora Bassa ★★★

The fishing here is said to be reminiscent of the glory days of Lake Kariba (Zimbabwe) in the 1960s, before it was overfished, and the **Ugezi Tiger Lodge** near Songo has all the boats, equipment and dining and accommodation facilities needed to make fishermen comfortable.

Independent anglers should head for **Chicoa**, nearby which you arrange to camp. About 10km (6 miles) before Songo, turn left onto a potholed road signposted **Estima E Chicoa** and carry on for 40km (25 miles) through Chicoa to the lakeshore. The Kapenta Fishing Association have *kapenta* (freshwater sardine) fishing camps near Chicoa and Mágoe.

## TETE TOWN

Tete must rank as the hottest town in southern Africa. Midsummer temperatures on the blistering banks of the Zambezi sometimes edge towards 50°C (122°F)! As the town's only swimming pool, at the river's edge next to the bridge, is usually empty, there is little in summer to recommend Tete as a stopover other than to eat an excellent meal at **Complexo Pemba**, refuel and buy fresh bread. To be fair, Tete does have a comfortable but overpriced motel, the **Motel Tete**, as well as a surprisingly lively nightlife, while for the historically minded there are two interesting sandstone stockades, one located just upstream from the bridge and the other in town next to the military garrison.

Tete may never become one of Mozambique's most visited places, but its location on one of Africa's busiest transport routes lends it great strategic importance. Until 1992 bandits often shot at travellers and truckers taking the short cut between Zimbabwe and Malawi via Tete, even though Zimbabwean soldiers protected this so-called Tete Corridor. Today the road is in top condition – police with radar speed traps are now the most serious hazard. Note that a negligible toll is payable on crossing the suspension bridge over the Zambezi into Tete, and that this is a favourite place to trap drivers who dare to exceed the 15kph (9½mph) speed restriction.

**Above:** *The bridge at Tete spans the Zambezi River.*
**Opposite:** *Roadside eateries, like this one on the road between Tete and Zóbuè, are a welcome sight.*

### BEAUTIFUL BIRDS

The unique mixture of varying geological components, soils, relief, altitude and precipitation in the **Manica** and **Tete** provinces have produced a unique habitat that is rich in endemic fauna and flora. Here birds such as the **green-headed oriole** and the **moustache warbler** draw birding enthusiasts from all over the world.

## From Beira to Tete at a Glance

### BEST TIMES TO VISIT

Avoid December to March when it is hot and humid, and coastal tropical cyclones are possible. The driest period in **Beira** (50mm; 2in rainfall per month), and lowest risk of malaria, is June to October. **Tete**'s weather and malaria situation is similar (without the cool breezes), but its monthly rainfall is only around half.

### GETTING THERE

**By Air**: Beira and Tete are served by LAM's domestic line, reservas@lam.co.mz www.lam.co.mz Maputo Central Reservations: (21) 46-5810, or Johannesburg: (11) 622-4889, fax: 616-5794.
**By Bus**: Transportes Oliveiras and Virginias buses (two days between Maputo and Beira).
**By Boat**: Uni-Feeder (Unicorn Lines), www.grindrod.com Weekly service linking Pemba, Nacala and Durban with Beira.
**By Road**: Varying surface tarmac roads from Maputo and Mutare. The EN1 has been extended (completed in 2003) between Inchope (EN6) and Caia (Zambezi ferry) via Vila de Gorongosa. From Zimbabwe, *chapas* (minibuses) link Beira with the border and other towns in this region.

### GETTING AROUND

City taxis (*tuksees*) are usually fairly dilapidated, but not cheap (US$15–20, airport to city). They meet flights at Beira airport and often wait outside the more expensive

hotels. Car-hire firms in Beira are **Avis**, tel: (23) 30-1263, fax: 30-1265, and **Hertz**, tel: (23) 32-2315, fax: 32-2415. Never leave a car unattended.

### WHERE TO STAY

Good accommodation is scarce, so book in advance.

### Beira
*LUXURY (SEMI)*
**Hotel Embaixador**, 203 Rua Major Serba Pinto, tel: (23) 323 121, fax: 323 788. Free airport transfers, room service, secure parking, conference facilities and a restaurant.
**Hotel Moçambique**, tel: (23) 325011, mozambhotel@ teledata.mz On Bagamoio Street, downtown – in front of the Hotel Tivoli. Air-con, pool.
**Hotel Tivoli**, 363 Avenida Bagamoio, tel: (23) 320300, fax: 320301, h.tivoli-beira @teledata.mz www.tivoli-beira.tdhotels.pt/tivoli/en Ideal for the business traveller; 24-hour room service and a good restaurant.

*MID-RANGE*
**Private Guest Houses**, Amigos Lda (Limitada), tel: (23) 311 915, Marion: +258 820 311 350, Dave: +258 825 575 030, kapensis@mango.zw
**Hotel Miramar**, Av. Matéus Sansão Muthemba, tel: (23) 32-2283. Close to beachfront.

*BUDGET*
**Bique's Restaurant and Campsite**, Av. FPLM, Macúti

suburb; booking office in Beira, tel: (23) 31-3051, fax: 32-7704. On beach, tatty ablutions, popular bar and restaurant.

### Savane Estuary
*MID-RANGE/BUDGET*
**Rio Savane**, 35km (22 miles) north of Beira, tel: (23) 323555, mobile: +82 385 7660. Transfers across the estuary from secure carpark. Camping and cottages. Good birding on pristine estuary with a deserted beach. Special.

### Chimoio
*LUXURY (SEMI)*
**Executive Manica**, tel: (51) 23135, fax: 23129; 500m off the main road behind the Feira Popular (FEPOM), pool (usually empty), air conditioning, TV, hot showers.

*BUDGET/MID-RANGE*
**Pink Papaya Backpackers**, tel: +82 237 2980, helenmlarge @hotmail.com www.hostelz. com/display.php/27960+The +Pink+Papaya Central.
**Residencial Flor de Vouga**, tel: (51) 22469, cnr Rua Dr Araujo de La Cerda and Av. 25 de Setembro above Banco Austral.

### Parque Nacional da Gorongosa
**Chitengo Camp**, www.carr foundation.org Basic furnished huts, shady camp site has ablution facilities with running cold (but not drinkable) water. Entrance Mt200,000, same per day for camping.

## From Beira to Tete at a Glance

### Manica
*MID-RANGE/BUDGET (CAMPING)*
**Casa Msika Resort**, Lake Chicamba, tel: (251) 22675, fax: 22701 in Chimoio; or Beira, tel: (23) 32-2796, fax: 32-4589. Comfortable rondawels with bedding, towels, soap; camp sites, pool and restaurant.

### Catandica
**Forest Retreat**, tel: mobile +82 237 2980, helenmlarge @hotmail.com Look for turn-off 6km north of Pungóè River bridge on E.N. 103. En-suite chalets, DSTV, meals can be arranged. Shady camp sites.

### Cahora Bassa/Songo
*LUXURY/MID-RANGE/BUDGET*
**Ugezi Tiger Lodge**, near Songo at Cahora Bassa dam wall, tel: Johannesburg (+27 11) 447 4747, 788 4724, info @sportfishafrica.co.za www. sportfishafrica.co.za Chalets (air-con), tents, camp sites and restaurant, boats for hire.

### Beira
**Bique's** (Beeky's), Estoril end of Av. FPLM, tel: (3) 31-3051. Huge menu, satellite TV.
**Restaurante Arcádia (Johnny's Place)**, Av. Poder Popular, tel: (3) 32-2266. A Beira favourite for 30 years.
**Take-Away 2+1**, 7 Rua 100, Maquinino (from Praça da India go up Av. 24 Julho and take the fourth left), tel: (3) 32-9883. A reputation for excellent Mozambican dishes.
**O Zequinha** (Clube Náutico

da Beira), Av. FPLM, tel: (3) 31-3093. Restaurant with pool; cool terrace overlooking the ocean.
**Moulin Rouge**, off the station parking area. Excellent Sunday lunches.

### Chimoio
**ELO 4**, Av. 25 de Setembro, no telephone. Mozambican/ Italian. Recommended.

### Manica
**Casa Msika**, Chicamba dam, tel: (51) 22675, fax: 22701 in Chimoio. Reasonably priced pub-restaurant.

### Tete
**Complexo Pemba**, on the riverfront upstream from the bridge. Simple menu, charming ambience with excellent meals – recommended.

**Venture Far**, based at Clube Nautico, offers boat charter, birding and accommodation. Contact Chris, tel: +846 820 200, Marion, tel: +846 820 210, venturefar@teledata.mz
**Gorongosa National Park** is open for self-sufficient visitors. Go to Songo and the Ugezi camp where boats can be hired. There is a ferry capable

of carrying a small vehicle from Ugezi Lodge (Songo) to Zumbo (Zambia/Zimbabwe border) and back twice per month; takes 2 days.

Professional up-to-date advice (fee payable) is available via www.mozguide.com Mike@mozguide.com
### Beira
**Acisofala** is an excellent business consultancy in the Manica building, 264 Av. Poder Popular, tel/fax: (23) 320335, acisofala@yahoo.com www.acisofala.com
**Internet Café at Telecommunicões (TDM)**, off the Praça do Município, downtown Beira and at Complexo Shoprite, Chimoio.
**LAM** (Air Mozambique), www.lam.co.mz tel: (23) 30-1021, fax: 32-8632.
**Tecnauto** (vehicle repairs), tel: (23) 21-2893 or 21-2993.
**Sabin Air Charter**, tel: (23) 30-1392, fax: 30-1393.
### Tete
**Hidroelétrica Cahora Bassa** (HCB), tel: (252) 20059 or 22779.
**Auto Reparadora de Tete**, Av. 25 Junho, tel: (252) 22581 or 23096.

| BEIRA | J | F | M | A | M | J | J | A | S | O | N | D |
|---|---|---|---|---|---|---|---|---|---|---|---|---|
| AVERAGE TEMP. °F | 84 | 80 | 79 | 77 | 75 | 72 | 72 | 73 | 77 | 80 | 82 | 84 |
| AVERAGE TEMP. °C | 29 | 27 | 26 | 25 | 24 | 22 | 22 | 23 | 25 | 27 | 28 | 29 |
| RAINFALL in | 11 | 9 | 10 | 4 | 2 | 1.5 | 1.2 | 1 | 0.7 | 1.2 | 6 | 10 |
| RAINFALL mm | 280 | 220 | 260 | 100 | 60 | 40 | 30 | 25 | 20 | 30 | 145 | 260 |

# 7
# North of the Zambezi

The rugged provinces of **Zambézia**, **Nampula**, **Cabo Delgado** and **Niassa** make up the area north of the **Zambezi River**. As evidenced by the 2001 floods, which displaced hundreds of thousands of people and prevented the Caia ferry from operating for weeks, the powerful Zambezi still forms a huge barrier to movement between and development of the northern provinces. This is mainly because there is no accessible road bridge over the river downstream from Tete – the 3.7km (2½-mile) converted **rail bridge** (built in 1934 and converted for road traffic in 1998) between **Sena** and **Morrumbala** being served by very poor tracks on either side. Now there are two new and reliable 22-ton vehicle ferries operating at Caia, while the Inchope–Gorongosa–Caia highway was completed in 2003. Contruction of a $85 million bridge across the Zambezi at Caia is due to be complete by 2009. Thus the mighty Zambezi that divides Mozambique into two distinct regions – a south influenced by South Africa and Zimbabwe, and a north which relates to Malawi and Tanzania – will no longer be a barrier to progress.

Until the late 19th century, the northern coast from **Chinde** to **Mocímboa da Praia** had most of the Portuguese government's attention. Apart from modest trading posts at Tete, Beira, Inhambane and Maputo Bay, the area south of the Zambezi was considered too far away from maritime trading routes to warrant extensive development. This was why former Lourenço Marques was declared the capital only in 1898. During the previous four centuries Ilha de Moçambique had been the principal city and busiest port.

---

**DON'T MISS**

**\*\*\* Ilha de Moçambique (Mozambique Island):** museums, 16th-century fortress, fascinating history.
**\*\*\* Ilhas das Quirimbas:** explore this remote and beautiful coral archipelago.
**\*\* Nampula to Lichinga:** stunning mountains on this breathtakingly scenic route.
**\*\* Praia da Wimbe (Pemba):** spend a week in a cosy bungalow.
**\* Zambezi delta:** very impressive, especially when viewed from the air.

---

**Opposite:** *The entrance to the Fortaleza São Sebastião on Ilha de Moçambique.*

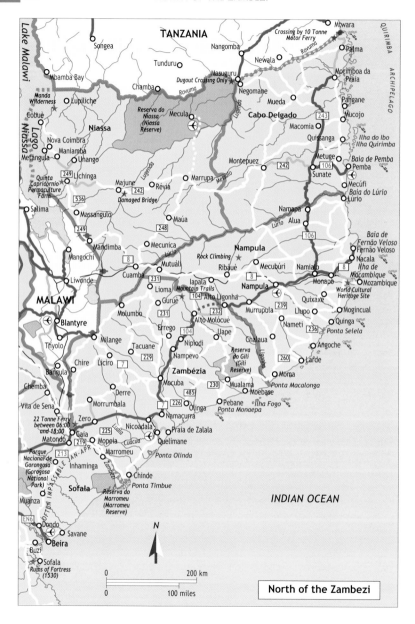

North of the Zambezi

**Left:** *Quelimane lies on the bank of the winding Rio dos Boas Sinais.*

## QUELIMANE

Quelimane (pronounced 'Kelimani') is one of Africa's few good river ports. It lies on the **Rio dos Bons Sinais** *(River of Good Omens)*, a name given to the mangrove-lined estuary by Vasco da Gama when he anchored there in 1498 on a mission to find a sea route to India. A *padrão* (stone pillar), erected at the river mouth to commemorate this landing, was claimed by the sea over 50 years ago. The river could also have been named Rio dos Sepulturas (River of Graves) as the first two Europeans to die in southern Africa were buried here, having succumbed to the combined ravages of scurvy and malaria.

Today over 200,000 people live in Quelimane, capital of Zambézia province, making it Mozambique's fourth-largest town. **Tea estates**, **coconut** and **cashew farms** on the coastal flats are the main providers of rural employment, while city dwellers manage to exist by trading, manufacturing and working in ventures that have survived decades of isolation. Most people live in the lively, colourful *bairros* that stretch for some distance out into the coconut plantations.

Main tribal groups are the Lómwè, Chuabo, Marende and Sena. Similar to the Tsonga and Shangaan of southern Mozambique (refugees from King Shaka's reign of terror nearly two centuries ago), the Chuabo people clustered deep in the fever-ridden mangrove swamps around Quelimane for protection against the Mwenu Mutapa.

### CLIMATE

Most of the area has a **tropical** climate; Due to its higher altitude, **Lichinga** in Niassa is somewhat cooler. The **wet** and **humid** months are from **November** to **April**, when temperatures rarely drop below 20°C (68°F), and often reach 40°C (104°F). **Summer rainfall** tops 200mm (8in) monthly at Quelimane, Pemba and Nampula, 300mm (12in) during March at Lichinga, and 500mm (19in) during January at Gurúè. **June** to **August** are the **cooler** and **drier** months.

### THE WINDS OF NIASSA

For the *marinheiros* (sailors) of *Lago Niassa* (Lake Malawi), a thorough understanding of the language of the lake winds can mean the difference between calm and calamity: the 'Vuma' comes from the north at storm strength, ripping off the roofs of houses on its way. 'Muela' winds from the south capsize dhows and bring malaria, while 'Lichinga' can come from either the north or the south, bringing heavy rains in its wake. And that large undulating cloud? This is the 'Vumi', a plague of flying insects, collected and cooked by the lake people.

**Above:** *Zalala Beach, once considered by Sir Malcolm Campbell for an attempt to break the land-speed record.*

### Quelimane Harbour ★

Quelimane is the terminus of the 96km (60-mile) railway from **Mocuba**, which is not in operation at present. From the station, a narrow-gauge line runs to the two concrete-and-steel jetties *(caias)* where steam engines once shunted goods to and from the harbour. Here the Rio dos Bons Sinais is 1.6km (1 mile) wide, and its nine-knot current, treacherous shifting sandbanks and 3.5m (11ft) tidal range make Quelimane harbour difficult to navigate. A century and a half ago, the Royal Navy brigantine *Dart*, sent to pick up **David Livingstone**, sank on the sandbar lying across the river mouth, resulting in the loss of eight crew members. Today the river is constantly dredged to provide passage for the coasters seeking cargoes of copra, fish and rice. A new berth for fishing trawlers, as well as refrigeration facilities, have recently been completed 2km (1¼ miles) from Quelimane.

### Zalala Beach ★★

At the end of a tarmac road north from Quelimane, which runs through an endless forest of coconut trees, you will discover Zalala beach and enormous succulent **prawns**. Dragged in by the local fishermen, **barracuda** (*Sphyraene barracuda*), squid or **bluefin kingfish** (*Caranx melampygus*) may also appear in the nets. Praia de Zalala lies wide and flat and, because it is so isolated, resembles a lost runway for some forgotten aircraft. The beach is long and hard-packed enough to have been considered for one of Sir Malcolm Campbell's attempts at breaking the world land speed record. Should you own a **land yacht**, bring it to Zalala and sail off into the sunset.

**Zalala town** consists of a small group of holiday houses and a basic restaurant with a bar and dance floor, and is flanked by little fishing villages.

## The Zambezi Delta

This delta, a remote unspoiled wilderness of shifting sand islands, savanna and mangrove trees, is one of the few places in Mozambique where big game (elephant, buffalo, lion and roan antelope) still occurs. **Chinde**, a small port on the deepest tributary, was once busy with cranes loading sugar into cargo ships. Cyclones have almost obliterated the site of old Chinde, and a new town was built further inland. A light rail system once linked Chinde to the newly revived Marromeu Sena sugar estates further upriver on the banks of the Zambezi.

The best way to view the 1500km² (579 sq mile) expanse of channels and islands is from the air. Three **air charter** companies are based in Beira and it is fairly inexpensive to hire a light plane for a low-level flyover of the delta. Unique Air in particular have, in the past, been reliable. You can fly in, land at Chinde and spend a few days exploring the railways before you are picked up again (by prior arrangement), or enjoy an **aerial wildlife-spotting safari** over the delta habitat – by far the cheaper option.

## Nampula

In 1967 the Portuguese, in the face of Frelimo's growing disenchantment with **colonial rule**, established Nampula as their main military base. Its location on the important **Nacala–Malawi railway** and on the north–south overland route contributed to attach to Nampula the label: 'capital of the north'. Despite its isolation it is an important service centre for the surrounding area and provides essential amenities. Diesel and petrol (unleaded due end 2006) are available, there is cellphone reception, supermarkets and a wide range of accommodation. Because LAM and Air Corridor scheduled flights land here regularly and there are daily trains from Cuamba (near Malawi), Nampula is the traveller's hub of the north. It has a hospital,

### The Shrinking Delta

When Livingstone arrived at Quelimane in 1856, the river port on the **Rio dos Boas Sinais** still lay on the northern edge of the wide Zambezi delta. In the south, the delta extended down to the mouth of the Luauá River, making it over 200km (124 miles) wide. Regulation of the turbulent floodwaters by upstream dams at Kariba and Cahora Bassa has effectively weakened the Zambezi's output and reduced the delta to half its natural size.

**Below:** *Traditional Makua huts like this occur in Nampula province.*

**Above:** *A rock climber's paradise – the granite outcrops in Nampula province.*
**Opposite:** *The entrance to the port captain's villa on Ilha de Moçambique.*

---

**STREET OF FIRE**

Luis Camões, 16th-century poet and historian, lived for a decade on **Ruo do Fogo** (Street of Fire), frequented by prostitutes. For him, it embodied the flaming passion that lonely sailors had for the island's beautiful women. He wrote: 'Seen from the sea, or a bird's eye view... the island is a unique woman, lying sensuously in a state of abandon, in a sea of colours, sun-worshipping on the beach.' It is fitting that Camões' statue still stands on a small *praça* in front of an immaculately restored house called Casa Branca, which would have been standing during his lifetime.

---

public telephones, *migração* (visa extensions) and a well-stocked **municipal market**. The **Clube CVFM** (Railway Club) is even able to offer a swimming pool with clean water, though they do tend to charge the earth for the privilege of using it.

### The Quelimane–Nampula Road **

From Caia, as far as **Namacurra** (a little outpost without a fuel station), the road has been re-tarred, as has the 37km (23-mile) deviation to Quelimane from **Nicoadala**. In **Mocuba**, you'll find an enigmatic signpost pointing to various places, none of which is **Alto Molócuè**, your next objective. Despite sometimes being virtually cut off from the south due to the flooding Zambezi preventing access to the Caia ferry, Mocuba is surprisingly busy, with a service station, an Olympic-size public swimming bath and a vast, open-air *mercado*.

The 258km (162 miles) of the EN104 between Mocuba and Alto Ligonha via Alto Molócuè appear benign at first, but watch out! A little after the turn-off to **Errego**, 100km (62 miles) out of Mocuba, there is a sudden deviation (the first of four) to the left, the smooth tarmac road continuing on to an abrupt dead end. If you're driving at night, you may discover this anomaly by ending nose-first in mud! If you zero your odometer at Mocuba, the deviations are at 100km (62 miles), 125km (78 miles), 140km (87 miles), 171km (106 miles) and at 277km (173 miles). To avoid any disasters on this route, keep looking well ahead: bush flattened on the roadside by vehicles constantly having to take evasive action is an indication of trouble ahead.

Between Caia and Nampula lies a pristine stretch of **miombo forests**, **clear streams** and prolific **bird life** on this, one of Africa's most remote overland routes. However, do not underestimate the realities of travelling on roads which disappear unexpectedly in a region where fuel, spares and repair services are unknown and heavy rain can leave you stranded between flooding rivers!

## ILHA DE MOÇAMBIQUE (MOZAMBIQUE ISLAND)

Ilha de Moçambique is located where the Mozambique Channel is at its narrowest and Madagascar is only 350km (217 miles) to the east – one of the reasons why first the Arabs and later the Portuguese turned it into a major **fortified port city**. Other features favouring over a thousand years of foreign occupation are a **safe anchorage** and fortunate location in relation to the monsoonal trade winds.

Though the **Arabs** probably began trading with East Africa around AD500, the formal documentation of their 1500-year dominance in this sector of the Indian Ocean was not a Portuguese priority. What is certain is that sultans held sway in this area when Portuguese explorer **Vasco da Gama** steered his 150-tonne caravel into the calm waters off the island in 1498.

This tiny isle (known simply as Ilha), just 2500m (8202ft) long and 600m (1969ft) at its widest point, is a **microcosm** of the major religious tribal, cultural and linguistic influences which have formed modern Mozambique. The island has been dubbed Africa's 'meeting point of civilizations'. Persians, Indians and Arabs came to trade, and stayed; the Portuguese settled for 500 years; the Dutch and the English tried, in vain, to dislodge them (had the Dutch succeeded, Cape Town would not exist); and today people still stop over on fishing expeditions.

Early commerce centred on cloth, beads and spices from the East which were bartered for **ivory**, **gold**, **precious stones** and **slaves** from the African hinterland. Eager to

### 'MISSANGA DO MAR'

The currency of trade during Arab times was porcelain and gold trading beads. Belligerent newcomers to the island, the Portuguese sank many Arab vessels near Ilha de Moçambique during the **trade war** (1498–1504). Today the beads are still washing ashore. Along with modern plastic and glass baubles, *missanga* are threaded onto fishing line to make necklaces to sell to visitors.

### MOZAMBIQUE'S NATIONAL MUSEUM OF ETHNOLOGY

Situated on the bottom end of Nampula's Av. Eduardo Mondlane, next to a cinema, the **Museu Nacional de Etnologia** is housed in a marble neoclassical building, once the governor's palace. Artefacts from all over the country provide a fascinating insight into the country, both past and present. Behind the museum is a Makonde co-operative where carvers sit and get on with their trade, while their children bash out tunes on timbila marimbas (traditional xylophones).

share in (and dominate) the ancient trade routes, King Emanuel of Portugal sent out scouts to blaze a trail to India. Nine years after Vasco da Gama clashed with Arab sultans on the island, the Portuguese formally occupied it, building a small **stockade** and leaving behind a mere 15 men to protect this outpost.

### Fortaleza São Sebastião ★★★

In 1558, using granite quoins shipped as ballast from Portugal on the light caravels, construction on the fortress of St Sebastian began. Due to the lengthy voyage to and from the motherland, the 12m (39ft) high, 750m (2460ft) long walls of the fortress were completed only 40 years later. For years São Sebastião was Africa's largest structure south of the Sahara, meant to symbolize the impregnable foothold of the Portuguese in Africa. However, it took the economic realities of the 20th century, not foreign invaders, to finally dislodge the settlers. Bigger modern ships needed deeper ports, and isolation, long an asset, now became an impediment. By 1960, the island had lost all of its former importance to the Portuguese and was left to rot.

### Capela de Nossa Senhora do Baluarte ★★

This church, which lies in ruins behind the fortress on the northeastern point of the island, was built in 1503. Although brutally vandalized and severely dilapidated, if you look inside you will see a crumbling memorial tablet.

### Palácio de São Paulo (Museus da Ilha) ★★★

Originally built in 1619 to house the island's governor and administration, St Paul's Palace is now a **museum** and has been declared a **World Heritage Site**. Recently the huge funding required to turn around some 50 years of neglect has started to trickle in and the curator, James, has restored the building as well as the beautifully carved **Goanese** furniture, **Portuguese** oil paintings, fragile **Chinese** pottery and porcelain, and the **Indian** tapestries and **Arab** drapes previously damaged by the badly leaking roof. There is a good information centre with maps and booklets and the museum is open daily from 08:00–12:00 and again from 14:00–17:00.

### Chocas-Mar ★★

On an enticing beach looking out onto **Baia da Condúcia**, once a resort for affluent Nampula residents, some of the holiday homes at Chocas-Mar have been renovated and a small resort has opened. The road is in fairly good condition, and when you get to **Mossuril** you will need to ask for directions to get there. Apart from the fine beach at Chocas, **Mossuril Bay** is favoured by mating **southern right whales** from July to October each year, a spectacle well worth the journey. Since it is difficult to book accommodation, it is best to arrive during the week – the weekends are popular with people from Nampula and Nacala.

With a population of about 14,000, the village section (Bairro Makúti) of Ilha de Moçambique is one of the most densely populated places in Africa. There are no ablution facilities, so the beaches are used as public toilets. If you're keen to suntan, take a dip or snorkel, rather catch a dhow or go with Dugong Dive to the nearby Goa or Snake (*Das Cobras*) islands where the sand and the sea are clean.

**Opposite:** *The 16th-century Capela de Nossa Senhora do Baluarte overlooks the sea.*
**Below:** *This bandstand graces the square in front of the Palácio de São Paulo.*

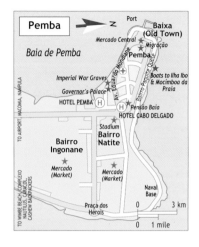

Pemba

Baia de Pemba

Port
Baixa
(Old Town)
Mercado Central
Migração
Pemba
Imperial War Graves
Boats to Ilha Ibo & Mocimboa da Praia
Governor's Palace
HOTEL PEMBA (H)
(H) Pensão Baia
HOTEL CABO DELGADO
Stadium
Bairro Natite
Bairro Ingonane
Mercado (Market)
Mercado (Market)
Naval Base
Praça dos Herois
TO AIRPORT, MACOMIA, NAMPULA
Av. Eduardo Mondlane
Bairro Pemba Que...
TO WIMBE BEACH, COMPLEXO NAUTILUS, CARACOL, CASHEW BACKPACKERS

0    3 km
0    1 mile

**Opposite:** *Board games are the speciality of this little workshop in Pemba.*
**Below:** *The idyllic sand and sea of Pemba's popular beach, Praia da Wimbe.*

## PEMBA

Before 1975, Pemba, the capital of Cabo Delgado province, was called **Porto Amelia**. The residents have dubbed it Mozambique's **papaya paradise**, which is fairly apt, as this little port is located on a headland squeezed between a magnificent inland bay and an idyllic beach where tall papaya trees lend their shade.

Although most visitors fly into Pemba on LAM, the 526km (326-mile) stretch of road between Nampula and Pemba has been completely re-tarred and is now passable in an ordinary car.

Seen from the bay, the white, flat-roofed buildings of Pemba's old town are typical of many of Africa's original colonial towns. Built on a hill, the town climbs steeply from the quayside to the Art Deco cinema at the top of the hill. Pedestrians are well looked after by flights of marble steps which allow shortcuts across the corners of the 'switchback' roads. These begin next to the municipal market (in the *Baixa*) and climb steeply, crossing half a dozen streets, before ending near the **Migração** building, where your visa can be extended if necessary.

Pemba's scenic *Marginal* (**promenade**) runs parallel to the mouth of the bay, before swinging right onto the main avenue to the airport and out of town. At a traffic circle overlooked by the **Banco Comercial de Moçambique** and **Hotel Cabo Delgado**, a turn up the hill will take you onto **Avenida Eduardo Mondlane**, the main thoroughfare to Pemba's more modern uptown quarter *(cima)*. Also on Eduardo Mondlane, you will find an art gallery, two supermarkets, **Viatur Travel Agency** (offering excursions, accommodation and car hire), a video rental, a hairdresser, a *pastelaria* (confectioners) and a *capulana* shop. The **governor's residence** is on the left and at the top of this avenue, from where you can enjoy a panoramic view of the bay and sea.

> ### Pemba Bay
>
> Pemba is reputed to be the world's largest inland bay. Its entrance is only about 2km (1½ miles) wide, opening up to a beautiful blue expanse of water with an area of around 375km$^2$ (144 sq miles) and a uniform depth of approximately 24m (79ft). During World War II, it is rumoured that sympathizers provided German U-boats (submarines) with supplies here.

### Traditional Markets ★★★

Around Pemba (and most large towns in Mozambique) are the *bairros*, which were referred to as 'native quarters' in colonial days. Pemba's most colourful *bairro,* Paquite Quete (pronounced 'pakiti-ket'), sits under coconut palms in a former mangrove swamp between the bay mouth and the docks. Here, in an area the size of a few football fields, fishermen, boat-builders, basket weavers, carpenters, traders, mechanics, smugglers, jewellers, mothers and children go about their business. There are *quiosques* and mosques, schools and traditional healers, but it is at the *bazares* (markets), such as Mbanguia, where you'll find Mozambique's lively soul (at a negotiable price).

Only about 20 or 30 minutes' walk away, other *bazares* worth investigating are in *bairros* **Natite** (just off Av. Eduardo Mondlane), **Ingonane** and **Cariáco** (on the way to Wimbe beach, before Heroes' Square), and **Wimbe**, inland from **Praia da Wimbe**. Trust a local to show you around and you will venture where few foreigners have been before. Enquire about the *esculturos* (sculptors) at the **Cooperativo Makonde**, en route to Wimbe beach just before the Praça dos Heróis, which sports a statue of a Frelimo soldier, crafted from hardwood.

**Above:** *This picture-perfect little villa is on Ibo Island.*
**Opposite:** *The old Fortaleza de São João Baptista is but a ruined shadow of its former self.*
**Below:** *A silversmith at work in Ibo Island's fort.*

## AROUND PEMBA

Pack a picnic lunch and head for glorious **Chuiba beach**, a little way past Wimbe beach. The peaceful solitude and clear water make up for the lack of facilities. The folk at **Russell's Place** and the inhabitants of the fishing village nearby are friendly, but petty theft is a problem.

Hire a 4WD vehicle from Kaskazini (*see* p. 121) and tour around the bay, through coastal forests, to **Metuge** village, and **Pangane** beach 125km (78 miles) further. You can motor out to quaint **Mecúfi** fishing hamlet, 35km (22 miles) south of Pemba, or hire a boat from C.I. Divers based at **Complexo Náutilus**.

### Ibo Island ★★★

Ibo is just one of over 30 coral islands that form the **Arquipélago das Quirimbas**, stretching for some 250km (156 miles) from Ilha Mefunvo in the south to Ilha Tecomaji in the north. Mentioned in 8th-century Arab writings, the Portuguese only arrived some 700 years later. The Arabs had chosen the island for settlement because it was easy to defend against the 'sackers' from Madagascar. Initially one of the country's most affluent populations, Ibo's settlement was elevated to the status of town in 1761.

Construction of fortifications on Ibo commenced in 1754. The erection of the **Fort of São João Baptista** began 17 years later, and apparently took only a year to complete. Details of its construction are registered on two plaques, one above the fortified door, the other inside the entrance tunnel.

Ibo Island's formerly impressive mansions and magnificent villas mostly now lie roofless and in ruins.

## Quirimba Island ★

The Gessners, a family of German extraction, own coconut plantations on Quirimba Island as well as a delightful home. Quilálea marine sanctuary is nearby, reached via Quirimba's airstrip and a 20-minute boat ride.

## Pangane and the Ruvuma Ferry

Set under palms between two beaches meeting at a rocky point bristling with boababs, Pangane village offers *'Senhor Sookee' (Chung Sique)*, with a shop and rooms for hire, and Ishmael, who runs a camp near the point. If going north from here by car, you need to know if the new Ruvuma Ferry is operational (otherwise crossing is by dugouts), and the folk at Kaskazini (Pemba) should know, so e-mail: info@kaskazini.com

## Mueda ★

A momentous event occurred at Mueda in 1964, setting in motion formal resistance to Portuguese rule. Makonde elders, rebelling against the confiscation of their land by the settlers, attended a meeting with the Portuguese governor here and hundreds of them were machine-gunned during an ensuing riot. Today the town has a memorial to the Mueda Massacre.

## Reserva do Niassa and Lago Niassa (Lake Malawi) ★★★

Known as 'Africa's last true wilderness', the **Niassa Reserve**, at 38,000km² (14,668 sq miles), is the largest game reserve in Mozambique. Surprisingly it has over 12,000 elephant, 8000 buffalo, and with around 200 animals, is one of the last refuges of the highly threatened wild dog (*lycaon pictus*). **Lago Niassa** has wild beaches such as Chuanga near Metangula and Nkwichi which is adjacent to a fledgling reserve near Cobúè called Manda Wilderness. Access (LAM flights) is via **Lichinga**, which has a charming farm inn called **Quinta Capricórnio**.

---

### FORTALEZA DE SÃO JOÃO BAPTISTA, IBO

This 18th century pentagonal fort had food storage, armouries and barracks for 300 troops. The entire population of the Island of Ibo and nearby Quirimba and Matemo sought refuge here during Arab, French, British and Dutch forays. From 1960–74 activists resisting Portuguese colonial rule were kept here as political prisoners. It is now a historical monument.

## North of the Zambezi at a Glance

Tropical cyclones can hit this stretch of **coastline** from December to March. The whole year is **hot**, with May to October being the **driest** months. The climate around Lichinga is modified by altitude, so winter nights can be bitterly cold.

**By Car**: Good access during dry season. Can be cut off during December–March. **By Air**: Quelimane, Nampula, Pemba and Lichinga are served by **LAM**, www.lam.co.mz **By Boat**: Uni-Feeder, **Unicorn Lines**, www.grindrod.com **Trains** go from Balaka (Malawi) to the Nayuchi/Entre Lagos border Mondays and Thursdays – truck transport to Cuamba. A train runs on alternate days from Cuamba to Nampula. **Buses** run from Blantyre's Stagecoach Bus terminus daily to Lichinga. **From Tanzania**: A ferry over the Rovuma, bridge being built near Negomano. **From Zimbabwe**: Buses run on the new road from Mutare and Beira to Quelimane.

Grupo Mecula buses operate from Quelimane and Nampula to all the main towns. In Nampula, contact **Moti Rent-a-Car**, tel: +258 26 218687, motimoz@ teledata.mz for sedans and 4WDs.

**Quelimane**
*LUXURY (SEMI)*
**Hotel Flamingo**, Av. 1 de Junho, tel: +258 24 21 5602, fax: +258 24 25 5023, grillo 13@virconn.com Pool, DSTV, air-conditioned en-suite rooms. Conference centre.

*MID-RANGE*
**Pensão Ideal**, Av. Filipe S. Magaia, tel: (24) 21-2739.

**Mutarara**
*BUDGET/MID-RANGE*
**Pensão Restaurante Mira Zambeze**, tel: (252) 24164.

**Mocuba**
**O Sítio**, Avenida da Junta. Clean rooms, shared bath.

**Alto Molócuè**
*BUDGET*
**Pensão Santo António**, off the *praça*; fans, meals, friendly. Or ask for the 'Quintinha'.

**Gurúè**
*MID-RANGE*
**Pensão Gurúè**, Av. Eduardo Mondlane, peter.pichler@ mail.austria.com

**Nampula**
*LUXURY*
**Girassol Hotel**, Nampula, tel: (26) 216000, girassolnampula hotel@visabeiramoz.co.mz

*MID-RANGE*
**Complexo Bamboo**, tel: (26) 216595, www.teledata.mz/ bamboo Chalets with air con, DSTV. Restaurant, bar, pool.

*BUDGET*
**Pensão Márques**, 12 Av. Paulo Samuel Kankhomba, tel: (26) 212527.

**Ilha de Moçambique**
*LUXURY*
**Hotel Omuhi'piti**, tel: (26) 640101, info@mocambique-set.com www.mocambique-set.com/produto.asp?id=89 Recently renovated, all the mod cons, BES.

*MID-RANGE/BUDGET*
**Casa Branca**, tel:+258 26 610066, mobile: +258 82 4543290, Flora204@ hotmail.com
**Patio dos Quintalinhos (Gabriel's)**, tel: +258 26 610090, www.mozambique guesthouse.com Swimming pool, private garden.

**Nacala**
*LUXURY/MID-RANGE*
**Hotel Maiaia**, tel: (26) 52-6351, fax: 52-6827, info@mocambique-set.com
**Bay Diving and Restaurant**, tel: (26) 520017, www.fimdo mundosafaris.com

**Pemba**
*LUXURY*
**Hotel Pemba**, tel Johannes-burg: +27 11 465 6904, fax: +27 11 465 9623, reservations@raniresorts.com www.pembabeach.com

*MID-RANGE*
**Complexo Naútilus**, tel: +258 272 21520 or +258 82 309777. Chalets overlook the

sweeping Wimbe beach. Recommended.

*BUDGET*
**Russell's Place (Caju Campismo)** backpackers & **Blackfoot Bar**, tel: +258 82 686273, Russellbott@ yahoo.com.au

*Quirimba Islands*
*LUXURY*
**Quilálea Island**, tel: (272) 21808, mobile: 82 3263900, quirimbas@plexusmoz.com www.quilalea.com Recommended.

*Ibo Island*
*MID-RANGE*
**Bela Vista Lodge**, www. wildlifeadventures.co.za

*Medjumbe Island*
*LUXURY*
**Medjumbi Island Resort**, www.raniresorts.com

*Guludo*
**Guludo Lodge**, www.guludo. com Luxury, isolated community tourism experience.

*Montepuez*
*MID-RANGE*
**Aurora 'Aos Corações do Mundo'** (To the Hearts of the World), tel: (272) 51300, aurora@teledata.mz or info@auxcoeurs-dumonde.org

*Cuamba*
*MID-RANGE*
**Hotel Vision 2000**, tel: (271) 62632, h-vision2000@ teledata.mz Air-con, BES.

*Lichinga*
*MID-RANGE*
**Girassol Lichinga**, tel: (27) 121 280, fax: 121 247, Av. Filipe Samuel Magaia, www.girassol hoteis.co.mz/en/ Newly built with Conference Room, restaurant/bar, air-con, pool and DSTV.

*Lago Niassa (Lake Malawi)*
*LUXURY*
**Nkwichi Lodge**, tel Malawi mobile: 82 709 792, +265 (0) 9 216 108, Satellite: +88 1631 5291 51, www.manda wilderness.org Perfect lakeside setting – foot safaris into the Manda Wilderness. Recommended.

*Quelimane*
**Pizzeria**, near the station.

*Nampula*
**Café Carlos**, tel: (26) 21-7960, off Rua dos Continuadores, tasty Italian. Recommended.

*Nacala*
**Bay Diving**, 10km down the Fernão Veloso road; *see* Where to Stay.

*Ilha de Moçambique*
**Relíquias** (Claudia), tel: (26)

61-0092. Landward side, near museum. Recommended.

*Pemba*
**Aquila Romana**, Italian, end of Wimbe beach.
**Pastelaria Flor d'Avenida & Gastronomia**, Av. Eduardo Mondlane. Capuccinos.

*Lichinga*
**O Chambo**, tel: (271) 21354, next to the Mercado Municipal. Worth the wait.

**Nampula**: Complexo Shoprite has imported goodies. Sunday *Mercado Artesanato* (craft market) near Hotel Tropical. **Ilha de Moçambique**: buy mementos at the Museum Information Centre. **Pemba**: Artes Makonde, Wimbe beach.

In Pemba, contact **Kaskazini**, tel: +258 82 30 96 990, info@kaskazini.com www.kaskazini.com **Pemba C.I. Divers**, scuba and boat hire: www.cidivers.com

**Kaskazini**: www.kaskazini.com **All things Mozambique**: www.mozguide.com

| NAMPULA | J | F | M | A | M | J | J | A | S | O | N | D |
|---|---|---|---|---|---|---|---|---|---|---|---|---|
| AVERAGE TEMP. °F | 79 | 77 | 79 | 75 | 73 | 72 | 72 | 73 | 77 | 80 | 82 | 80 |
| AVERAGE TEMP. °C | 26 | 25 | 26 | 24 | 23 | 22 | 22 | 23 | 25 | 27 | 28 | 27 |
| RAINFALL in | 10 | 9.8 | 7.5 | 4 | 1 | 0.7 | 0.7 | 0.5 | 1 | 1.2 | 1.5 | 5.5 |
| RAINFALL mm | 260 | 250 | 190 | 100 | 25 | 20 | 20 | 15 | 25 | 30 | 40 | 140 |

# Travel Tips

## Tourist Information

**Mozambique Tours**, Durban, South Africa, are reliable, professional and helpful; tel: (2731) 303 2190, mit@iafrica.com www.mozambiquetravel.co.za Mozambique has **diplomatic missions** in France, Germany, Italy, Portugal, the Russian Federation, the UK, Sweden, Switzerland and the USA. An excellent website covering all aspects of Mozambique with depth and authority is: www.mozguide.com **Public Information Bureau** (BIP), 772 Av. Francisco Orlando Magumbwe, Maputo, tel: (1) 49-0200, fax: 49-2622. BIP has a video room and reference library and sells books, magazines and maps.

## Entry Requirements

Apart from citizens of its neighbouring countries, all visitors need a **visa** – **passports** must be valid for at least six months after end of visit. In addition to your passport, two passport photos and photocopies of your passport must accompany your visa application. For US$30, visas are now always issued on entry (except at the Rovuma mouth border), but this can be time-consuming, so it could be better to obtain one in advance. Visitors arriving by vehicle must have a valid

driver's licence and the car's original **registration papers**. A temporary import permit (TIP) and MVA (third-party) insurance (called *seguros* – bought at the border) will be demanded at checkpoints all over the country. A good idea is to carry notarized (must be done in Mozambique) copies of your driver's licence and passport.

## Customs

If arriving by air, **electronic equipment** must be declared. Other consumable goods may attract import duties if their combined value is more than US$200 (per person), or if the official decides that you may sell them in Mozambique. **Pets** may be brought in from South Africa and Zimbabwe only if you have a vet's certificate indicating that they have had all their inoculations. You may have great difficulty bringing them back home.

## Health Requirements

Visitors from, or passing through, a **yellow fever** zone require a valid **International Certificate of Vaccination**. Cholera and smallpox vaccinations are not required, nor is there any form of AIDS screening for visitors. The tropical climate is ideal for *anopheles* mosquitoes, which transmit **malaria**. (Consult your physi-

cian before travelling into Mozambique.) **Bilharzia** in rivers and lakes and **AIDS** also pose serious threats for the foolhardy. Tap water is not potable, but many lodges and hotels have their own safe borehole water.

## Getting There

**By air: Maputo International Airport** is served by carriers from Europe (Paris and Lisbon), South Africa and Tanzania. **Pemba** has thrice-weekly and **Beira** receives one direct LAM flight from Johannesburg per week. **Vilankulo, Inhambane, Pemba** and **Mecula (Reserva do Niassa) Airports** (served by charter companies) are now 'airports of entry' and immigration services are available.
**By road:** Good tarmac roads lead from South Africa, Swaziland, Zimbabwe and western Malawi. The ferry over the Rovuma River runs at high tide only. **Luxury buses** from Johannesburg and Durban (South Africa) to Maputo daily. Contact Greyhound, www. greyhound.co.za tel: (+27 11) 276 8500 / (0)83 915 9000 or InterCape, www.intercape.co. za tel: +27 (0) 21 380 4400.
**By rail:** There are daily Spoornet Komati trains between Johannesburg and Komatipoort: www.spoornet.

co.za South Africa toll-free: 086 000 8888. Twice a week trains run from Balaka (Malawi) to Nayuchi/Entre Lagos; then get a lift to Cuamba from where there are trains on alternate days to Nampula.
**By boat:** Contact Grindrod, tel: +27 31 302 7911, www.grindrod.co.za/com panies_content.aspx?id=4

## What to Pack

Insect repellent, a sunhat and sunblock are essential. Long shirts and trousers help to ward off mosquitoes in the evenings. Beachwear may be daring, but off the beach women should cover up with a sarong, men with shirt and shorts. A warm jacket and trousers for winter evenings, an umbrella for the sudden tropical downpours and smart-casual evening wear for some restaurants and clubs.

## Money Matters

**Note:** Mozambique will rede-nominate the metical by 1000 to 1 (i.e. taking three zeros off), effective 1 July 2006. New coins and banknotes will be introduced on 1 July 2006 and the transitional period during which both old and new meticais can be used will last until 31 December 2006.
**Currency:** Unit of currency is the **metical** (MT), plural *meti-cais*. A 'quanto' or 'conch' (1000 meticais) is also referred to as *uma pão*. There are MT1000 and 5000 coins, while notes come in denominations of: MT1000; 5000; 10,000; 20,000, 50,000, 100,000 and 200,000. Stallholders in

markets and along the road don't carry much change.
**Exchange:** Money can be exchanged at banks, hotels and Mercados Secundário de Câmbios (Bureaux de Change) where you'll get best rates for US$ and SA Rand; other cur-rencies and travellers' cheques are difficult to change.
**Credit cards:** In Maputo, Beira and Chimoio, **Visa** cards can be used to draw the local equivalent of US$200 at Cirrus ATMs (so long as a PIN num-ber has been loaded onto the card), also at the more up-market hotels and restaurants in Maputo. Get a cash advance (up to the equivalent in *meticais* of US$500) from branches of the Banco Internacional de Moçambique (BIM). **Mastercard** holders can get cash from the Banco Austral, and use Cirrus ATMs if they have a PIN number.
**Traveller's cheques:** American Express Traveller's Cheques in US$ can also be exchanged at BIM ($15 appears to be the standard charge). Banks may charge commission per cheque, regardless of denomination.
**Tipping:** Waiters, porters, car guards (*guardas*) and other casual workers expect to be tipped. 10% for waiters, MT20,000 for the others.

## Accommodation

Outside of Maputo there are few five-star quality hotels, but comfortable **lodges** (from self-catering to full board) dot the coastline from Pontas do Ouro, Malongane and Mamóli in the south to the lodges on Ibo,

Quilalea and Medjumbe Islands in the far north. The small, quaint **boarding houses** (*pensãos*) range from the 'rather-sleep-in-your-car' variety to delightfully homely places where you can rest and recuperate. The supply of rea-sonably good and affordable accommodation cannot meet demand, and it is recom-mended that visitors book at least six months in advance to be assured of a room.

## Eating Out

The predominance and variety of seafood reflects Mozam-bique's maritime location. Restaurants range from pricey international (US$70 per meal) to simple sidewalk (US$3 per plate). Many establishments specialize in spicy Indo-Portuguese cuisine such as curries (*caril*) and grilled prawns (*camarão grelhado*), while market stalls may offer simple local fare like *mukhuwane* (spinach and shrimps). The variety of fresh produce on sale at the markets increases in the larger towns but is poor in the rural areas. Prices in Maputo and Pemba have become relatively high.

## Transport

**Air:** The capital cities of eight of Mozambique's 10 provinces (Inhambane and Xai-Xai excluded), are served by the domestic wing of LAM (Linhas Aéreas de Moçambique, www.lam.co.mz). Booking at least six months in advance is recommended. Air Corridor recently began operations: www.flyaircorridor.com

**Road:** The principal coastal road (Estrada Nacional 1, or **EN1**) which links Maputo, Xai-Xai, Inhambane, Vilankulo, Beira and northern Mozambique (the Caia ferry is operating reliably, and construction of the bridge has begun) has been, or is currently being, upgraded. Roads linking Mozambique to neighbouring countries have been repaired or are presently receiving attention. In the Zambézia, Nampula, Cabo Delgado and Niassa provinces, 4WD vehicles are essential during the rainy season (December–April).

**Road rules:** Although to the newcomer traffic will appear anarchic, *Moçambicanos* (should) drive on the left. Speed limit (strictly enforced using radar) within a built-up

area is 50kph (20mph), including sections of rural roads which simply pass a trading store. Outside urban areas, the general speed limit is 100kph (62mph).

**Car hire: Avis**, **Imperial** and **Europcar** are represented in Maputo and Beira, with **Imperial** in Nampula and **Moti Commercial** in Nacala. In Pemba, **Moti** sometimes has vehicles available for hire. Unless you are doing a round trip, you will have great difficulty hiring a vehicle.

**Overland visitors** driving their own vehicle are required to purchase **third-party insurance** (*seguros*) and temporary import permit (TIP) at the border; a carnet is not needed. Visitors are advised to carry a fully comprehensive travel and vehicle insurance and a **medical evacuation policy**, which can be issued by such organizations as Europ-Assist or Med-Rescue International. South of the Zambezi and in Nampula, fuel (diesel especially) is widely available and costs a little more than in South Africa. Diesel (*gasóleo*) is 20% cheaper than petrol (*gasolina*).

**Buses:** Coach services offering varying comfort and reliability link Maputo to Beira, stopping at all large towns in between. Try **Transportes Virginias** (Hotel Universo),tel: (1) 42-2225 or 42-7003, or **Transportes Oliveiras** (near Praça 16 de Junho), tel: (1) 42-1634 (both in Maputo).

**Trains:** Daily between Maputo and Marracuene, and on alternate days Nampula and Cuamba.

## ROAD SIGNS

*Direito* • Right
*Esquerda* • Left
*Paragem* • Bus stop
*Desvio* • Detour
*Controle* • Check-point
*Entrada proibida* • No entry
*Paragem proibida* • No stopping
*Rotatória* • Traffic circle
*Cidade* • City/town
*Sem saida* • Cul-de-sac
*Fechado* • Closed
*Covas* • Potholes
*Perigo* • Danger
*Posto Sanitário* • Health post
*Passagem* • Level crossing
*Entrada* • Entrance
*Saida* • Exit
*PPM* • Police station
*Obras* • Road works
*Avenida* • Avenue
*Rua* • Street
*Praia* • Beach

## Business Hours

Shops and offices usually open 07:30–12:30 and 14:00–18:30 Monday to Friday, and 09:00–13:30 and 15:00–18:30 on Saturday. Banks generally open from 80:00–15:00. Sidewalk *quiosques* (many are informal bars) stay open late at night.

## Time Difference

Mozambique is two hours ahead of Greenwich Mean (or Universal Standard) Time, one hour ahead of European Winter Time, and seven hours ahead of the USA's Eastern Standard Winter Time. Sydney is eight hours ahead of Mozambique. Ilha de Moçambique is far enough east for the sun to rise 1hr earlier (many visitors adjust their watches accordingly).

## Communications

Major towns have international public phone offices (*telecommunicações*), which are usually close to the post offices (*correios*), sometimes in converted, air-conditioned containers. **Dialling codes** (add '0' within Mozambique) are: Maputo 21; Xai-Xai 281; Beira 23; Chimoio 251; Quelimane 24; Tete and Songo 252; Nampula and Nacala 26; Lichinga 271; Pemba 272. Calls from province to province don't need a zero (0) at the beginning and within a province all eight digits are dialled. Calls from outside the country still need the country code 258 before the eight-digit number. To call a mobile from anywhere in Mozambique you no longer need a zero (0) at the beginning. Mozambique has two (regularly updated) telephone directories: *Zona Zul* for Maputo, Gaza and Inhambane provinces; *Zona Centro Norte* for the rest.
**Post offices** are open 07:30–12:30 and 14:30–16:30 Monday to Friday, but are closed over weekends.

## Electricity

Power supplied is 220 volts AC (50HZ), but as variations are common in Mozambique, appliances should be surge-protected. Socket types vary from 3- and 2-pin round to 2-pin square, so bring along a universal adapter plug.

## Weights and Measures

The metric system was introduced in the early 1960s. A pocket fisherman's spring balance is a very useful item.

## Health Precautions

The **tropical climate** carries with it a high incidence of insect as well as waterborne diseases and infection. Consult organizations dealing with **tropical diseases** for advice, bearing in mind that new strains of **malaria**, resistant to both chloroquine and pyrimethamine, occur throughout Mozambique. Enquire about the possible side effects of treatments such as Larium and take a trial dose a couple of weeks before departure. If staying for more than a week, take along a course of malaria treatment such as Coartem. Don't drink tap **water** unless the source is an uncontaminated borehole at one of the lodges. Boil all water or drink only the bottled variety, which is widely available but expensive. It is safest to assume that all lakes and rivers are infested with **bilharzia**, which is, however, fairly easily treated. Use **sun lotions** with the highest protection factor (Doxycycline, used as a malaria prophylactic, commonly causes mild to severe sun-sensitivity).

**AIDS** is rife in Mozambique and the usual precautions applicable elsewhere should be followed. Since blood at the hospitals may not have been screened properly for the HIV virus, opt for evacuation to South Africa if you need a blood transfusion. Stonefish, bluebottles, hammerhead and Zambezi **sharks** occur off the Mozambican coast. **Snakes** such as the deadly black mamba are not uncommon, but the chances of snakebite or shark attack are so small that they hardly warrant a mention. The bluebottle (or Portuguese man-of-war) belongs to a group of feeding polyps capable of inflicting a dangerous (but usually just very sore) sting.

## Health Services

Only in Maputo is adequate medical care available, and then at a price. If you are injured or become ill, you are strongly advised to make immediate use of your medical

---

### CONVERSION CHART

| FROM | TO | MULTIPLY BY |
| --- | --- | --- |
| Millimetres | Inches | 0.0394 |
| Metres | Yards | 1.0936 |
| Metres | Feet | 3.281 |
| Kilometres | Miles | 0.6214 |
| Square kilometres | Square miles | 0.386 |
| Hectares | Acres | 2.471 |
| Litres | Pints | 1.760 |
| Kilograms | Pounds | 2.205 |
| Tonnes | Tons | 0.984 |

To convert Celsius to Fahrenheit: x 9 ÷ 5 + 32

evacuation insurance and be transferred to one of Johannesburg's excellent private hospitals or to your home country. Although Mozambique's rural clinics are being refurbished, qualified doctors or other trained medical personnel may not be in attendance. Buy medications, including antibiotics, at a private *farmácia*.

## Personal Safety

In the larger cities such as Maputo, Beira, Pemba and Nampula, beware of pickpockets and don't venture into deserted or badly lit places at night unless you are with locals. Poverty is rife and so is petty thieving, but back-

packers and overlanders can relax at recognized camp sites which employ guards. Car hijackings and other armed robberies do occur, especially in Maputo and usually from the late afternoon onwards. Safe parking is scarce, but make an effort to seek it out, as vehicle parts, including windscreens and indicator lenses, are often stolen within minutes after you have left your vehicle. Groups of street children sometimes surround tourists and surreptitiously remove watches, wallets and other valuables from their unsuspecting victims. Without downplaying the horrific injuries that have been inflicted on Mozambicans by land mines, visitors who follow a few sensible precautions are far more likely to be stricken with malaria than come across **land mines**. A massive and thorough mine-clearing operation has already swept major roads, and is now concentrating on the minor ones and the more remote areas. Heed local knowledge, stick to well-used roads and trails, don't veer off – even for a call of nature – and you will be safe.

## Emergencies

Contact your embassy in the event of accident, vehicle theft or trouble with the law. If you run over someone, produce your third-party insurance (*seguros*) and accompany the police, who will have to arrest you for your own protection. Phone your embassy from the station. The police force and

ambulance service are generally poorly equipped and trained. In Maputo call the police at tel: (1) 42-7343 or 42-7575, and the fire brigade at tel: 198. For **private medical air rescue services** call Maputo: Netcare, Mike Ferguson.

## Etiquette

Mozambicans value good manners and courtesy. Modest dress is expected off the beach, but formal attire is rare. Request permission before taking photographs of people or entering private or communal property. Rather than paying any 'bribes', adopt a relaxed, friendly and unhurried attitude, which will confound unscrupulous customs officials.

## GOOD READING

• Newitt, Malyn (1994)
*A History of Mozambique.*
Wits University Press.
• Bartlett, Richard (Editor)
(1995) *Short Stories From
Mozambique.* Cosaw and
Ministerio da Educação,
Instituto Camões.
• Maclean, Gordon L (1996)
*Roberts' Birds of Southern
Africa.* John Voelcker Bird
Book Fund.
•Sinclair, Ian; Hockey, Phil &
Tarboton, Warrick (1995)
*Sasol Birds of Southern Africa.*
Struik Publishers.
• Moll, Eugene & Glen (1994)
*Common Trees of Southern
Africa.* Struik Publishers.
• Van der Elst, Rudy (1993)
*Common Sea Fishes of Southern
Africa.* Struik Publishers.